ADVANCE PRAISE FOR
YOU CAN'T BE EVERYWHERE

Anybody can call themselves an online marketing expert. Marie is the 'real deal' and treats marketing and conversion with the science and measurement it deserves.

— DAVID CARTER, EXECUTIVE DIRECTOR, INNOVATION FACTORY

Marie's advice is sound and her process and approach drives compelling results for business owners and entrepreneurs.

— ROB FARRELL, VP SALES AND MARKETING, SMARTPRINT

Marketing is often perceived as some kind of shadowy black magic performed by seers and visionaries and is one of the most misunderstood of all business functions. Marie's expertise combined with a sound programmatic approach takes the mystery out of digital marketing and creates consistent measureable results.

— JIM BARNETT, VP SALES AND MARKETING, PROMYS

Marie has developed and uses her proven methodologies to ensure clients marketing strategies are efficient, effective and evidence based.
— PETER WOOD, ENTREPRENEUR, CONSULTANT AND
FORMER PARTNER, ERNST & YOUNG CANADA

I've admired the work Marie has done for over a decade now. She has a pragmatic, proven approach to marketing that simply works. Marie cuts through all the "voodoo" to make sense of the programs and platforms you need to deliver results. This is a must read book.
— PETER EVANS, PRESIDENT AND FOUNDER, EXPERTFILE

In a sea of clutter and confusion, Marie has a sound approach that creates better results for business owners and entrepreneurs.
— RAY SIMMONS, PRESIDENT, DARCOR CASTERS

When it comes to digital marketing, Marie has an excellent understanding of the gap between what companies believe they need and what actually works with customers.
— DR. MIRA RAY, DIRECTOR, CENTRE FOR APPLIED
RESEARCH AND INNOVATION, GEORGIAN COLLEGE

Marie offers a refreshingly grounded perspective on how businesses should approach content marketing. There's no gimmick here. Her guidance is practical, validated, and viable.
— ANDY MCILWAIN, CONTENT & COMMUNITY AT GODADDY

Marie is uniquely qualified to understand the implications of today's digital marketing on the need for seamless integration between sales and marketing to drive growth.
— ANDREW FORD, PRESIDENT OF SALES
COPILOT AND SALES COPILOT ACADEMY

We have known Marie from the beginning of her journey into the digital marketing world. Her experience, insights and mentoring has allowed us to grow our business in ways we could not have imagined. Marie has the ability to know where one should be and when in the ever change digital landscape.

— ROS PLUMMER, CLEARMOUNT/SIGG NORTH
AMERICA, VP SALES & MARKETING

In what often appears as an ever-changing landscape of seller and buyer interactions in a digital world, Marie has a knack for boiling off the hyperbole and gets down to practical and effective strategies and tools to bring in the right prospects for big results.

— JOHN GRAHAM, EXECUTIVE VICE PRESIDENT, SOLUTIONS360

What awesome insight! Marie has an exceptional ability to distill complex information into a simple and strategic approach that drives real results. These concepts have been proven in hundreds of small business to implement revenue growth.

— LISA KEMBER, SERIAL ENTREPRENEUR AND
REGIONAL DIRECTOR, CONSTANT CONTACT

Marie has an uncanny ability to find "the signal in the noise" for those wanting to market in this complex new age of content-driven multi-channel digital marketing. I'm a big fan of her capabilities.

— LARRY KEATING, FOUNDER AND CEO, NPC
DATAGUARD AND KEATING TECHNOLOGIES

With all the online noise about digital marketing, Marie's no non-sense approach brings clarity and concise actions that can be taken to better improve your online efforts.

— EDWARD WENSING, AGENCY PRINCIPAL,
CANADIAN WEB SOLUTIONS

Marie brings innovative insights and leading edge approaches that are applicable to firms big and small who need help in defining their digital marketing strategies. She articulates her ideas in an engaging and insightful manner and the overall methodology just makes practical sense.
— DR. ANDREW AZIZ, DIRECTOR OF STRATEGY, METHODOLOGY AND QUANTITATIVE FINANCE, IBM ANALYTICS

Marie Wiese is a true digital marketing visionary, and one of the nation's foremost experts in defining, mapping and optimizing the customer journey, and growing businesses with sophisticated insights, techniques and technologies. Companies big and small, non-profits and senior government leaders have long sought Marie's wisdom in architecting truly disruptive content strategies with outsized and immediate market impact.
— CHRIS HOOK, SENIOR DIRECTOR OF GLOBAL MARKETING AND PR, ADVANCED MICRO DEVICES

Wisdom in a rapidly evolving and changing world—hard to come by. Marie has it, exercises it and makes it happen for her clients—digital marketing mastered.
— CHRIS HOWARD, PRESIDENT AND CEO CROSSFUZE

Marie's knowledge and foresight in the digital marketing space is second to none—Her insights on buyer personas are second to NO ONE!
— IAN TARRANT, DIRECTOR, CONTACT CENTRE OPERATIONS, MCAP

Running a business profitably means connecting to your customers in a visceral way. Marie has a proven track record in helping entre-preneurs to attract and retain customers by deploying engaging and sticky content marketing strategies.
— DON LONEY, PRESIDENT, LONEY PUBLISHING GROUP LTD.

Marie provides thoughtful and pragmatic direction in Digital Mar-keting, discover for yourself!
— TEDDE VAN GELDEREN, PRESIDENT, AKENDI

You Can't Be Everywhere is a powerful toolkit for pinpointing your smartest digital marketing priorities. Marie Wiese cuts to the chase with timely myth-busting, lucid advice and a step-by-step approach to driving bottom-line results.
— JEANETTE HANNA, BRAND MARKETER

I have had the pleasure of working with Marie for a number of years. Her passion for her customers' success and deep understanding of what it takes to get the heart of the buyer makes her a truly out-standing marketer.
— NIKKI GORE, SIREN MARKETING

YOU CAN'T BE EVERYWHERE

YOU CAN'T BE
EVERYWHERE

• • • • • •

A Common Sense Approach to Digital Marketing For Any Business

Marie Wiese

LIONCREST
PUBLISHING

CONTENTS

INTRODUCTION

* * * * *

A COMMON-SENSE APPROACH TO DIGITAL MARKETING

When I was kid, I had the pleasure of spending summers with my grandmother—one of the most creative people I have known. She wasn't an artist or a designer. When I say she was creative, I mean she was practical and could always invent a common-sense way of fixing a problem. There were lots of little touches throughout her house that were uniquely suited for the task at hand. She invented the retractable paper towel holder long before they were selling them at Walmart.

When I was ten years old, on one particular visit she gave me her 1960s Japy Script typewriter to use. I sat down to type on it and immediately became stumped about what to write. I had the tools and blank sheets of paper, but I was puzzled about what to commit to the page. I didn't have an audience. I didn't have a theme. I didn't have content. So instead of just typing randomly, my ten-year-old self figured out how to discover audience, theme, and channel for my content. I didn't realize it at the time, but I was setting myself up for a career in marketing.

After years of working in marketing for various people and companies, I was still struggling with messaging and content. It felt to me as if the world was getting more cluttered and confusing; and despite my best efforts as a marketer and business person, the advent of the Internet, social media, and content marketing made me feel as if I was ten years old again and staring at a blank typewriter.

Fast-forward to 2013 when I received the best piece of business advice I could possibly imagine. Perhaps it's something you already know. Ready? Here it is: You can't be everywhere. It's just not possible. And trying to be everywhere? It's hurting your business. Trying to be everywhere has a nasty side effect. You water down your impact on your audience when you try to force-feed it into any available channel.

In today's world of the 24-7 Internet, social media, and mobile phones, there is an abundance of places for you to be. And it's not just you—it's all of us. We're constantly trying to reach out through all of these channels and do all of these things for our business *and* in our personal lives. I just don't think you can try to be everywhere and still do any of it well.[1]

You've come to this book because you have a website for your business and you wonder why it's not working for you—or if it's working at all. You may feel as if there are too many choices available to you in terms of what you should be doing to market your company better, but it's all too overwhelming when you try to think about what to do next. Perhaps you've spoken with too many marketers who have confused you, or said something like, "Well, go try this"—and then when it doesn't work, they suggest something else.

The reason you're coming to a book like this is because you've tried something and it didn't work, and you don't know why. You're frustrated because you feel as if you're getting left behind. You're frustrated because you think you should be doing all sorts of things, but when you try to do them, they don't stand out and you don't get the results that you're looking for.

1   In Kevin Kelly's book *The Inevitable: Understanding the 12 Technological Forces That Will Shape Our Future*, he notes that the total number of web pages, including those that are dynamically created upon request, exceeds 60 trillion. That's almost 10,000 pages per person alive. When companies like ABC and then-start-up Yahoo! talked about content for web channels in the 1980s, they predicted there would be 5,000 channels available. That was an incredible number back in 1988. Instead what has happened is that billions of users have created content online. There are 500 million channels out there now—not a mere 5,000. Still think you can be everywhere?

I'm going to help you build a modern marketing program that takes out all of the guesswork. It's a simple approach based in common sense. Throughout this book, I will help you lay out a road map for what you need to do and what needs to change. A modern marketing program is built around the idea that you should spend as much time on the front end, understanding your customer journey, as you do on the back end, executing tactics.

FOCUS ON THE TYPEWRITER AND A BLANK PIECE OF PAPER

There's this overwhelming urge to do it all and be everywhere, as if that's what is going to get results. But in fact, if you just focus on good content and on making connections with the right people at the right time, you'll be further ahead than those who try to do it all.

There is a culture now that is built around trying to get involved in every channel or thinking there is one we simply have to pursue. Maybe this sounds familiar: "If I just spend a lot of money and have tons of pay-per-click support with Google Adwords, I'm going to double the growth of my business." But many people have come to the realization that this is just not true. Just because you keep sending your ad to the top of page one on Google, doesn't mean you're going to get the traction you want. There's a whole pile of other things that have to happen for you to get any goodness out of that from a sales perspective. But if you're not doing any of those other things particularly well, you haven't really understood what your customer wants and what kinds of content they need from you to make a decision.

In this book I'm going to lay out a simple approach for you to create great content that your customers will love, a well thought-out strategy that makes you a leader in your industry, and a common-sense approach to digital marketing. You'll spend less time spinning your wheels and more time focusing on what matters: your customers. It's all about having the common sense to stand in your customers' shoes to understand what they want from you—not the other way around.

A QUICK STORY

I want to tell you a story about a business I'll refer to as The ABC Company. The ABC Company thinks the only thing that matters in email marketing is how big they can make their list. It's all about the number of people they can get to sign up. There was a time in marketing when it was a numbers game—when it was about the number of ad impressions and mass reach. But I have now worked with lots of small businesses who would rather have 1,000 really engaged people who are not unsubscribing, who are opening emails on a regular basis, who are clicking through, and who are doing something as a result, than 10,000 names who opt out and bounce. But The ABC Company thinks that if they can just reach out to as many people as possible, it's going to improve their sales. Sadly, that's not necessarily true.

I've worked with clients who have said to me, "I just want more lead volume on my website." It's all about volume. But a funny thing happened when we improved their lead volume. You can easily buy your way into that game, but for The ABC Company (and many others who try this method) it was the wrong types of leads. Until you roll up your sleeves and understand who your best customers are, why they are buying from you, how they express your value proposition, and why they think you're valuable, you're just doing a bunch of superfluous things that don't generate action for you as a business. You're just typing onto a typewriter and you don't know what or why.

Regardless of what business you're in—whether you're selling a $100K piece of machinery or you have a $5 item on Amazon—your customers want to self-serve, they want to self-select, and they want to be able to do business with you in a way that is as easy as sitting in their pajamas at home on an iPad. The fact of the matter is we expect a certain level of professionalism, content, and good value when we hit somebody's website.

There was a time when CEOs would say to me, "Nobody's ever going to go look at my website before they buy from me." Now, that's just not true. Have you ever tried to visit a restaurant website on your phone and suddenly found yourself faced with menu PDFs buried deep into the site structure, no phone number or street address to be found, or worse yet, everything done completely in Flash? Chances are, they probably didn't get your business.

We recently received a grant from the National Research Council in Canada, where Marketing CoPilot is based. The survey was conducted in conjunction with Georgian College, just north of Toronto. We ran a research study called "What Makes a Good Website?" We surveyed buyers of services and sellers of services.[2]

Using the research, we were able to validate assumptions we had made about website usage. Funny enough, the biggest thing we learned is that the online survey tool we used was terrible. People commented that they hated taking the survey because the web experience was so bad. When considered alongside the data we collected, this proves the point about how important it is to have a good user experience on the web.

....

2   Read the report here:
     http://marketingcopilot.com/digital-marketing-research-report-request-2016/

This expectation to be everywhere has escalated to an all-time high thanks in large part to social media. It's this alone that makes us feel as if we can be everywhere, connect with everyone, and broaden our outreach like never before. But in feeling this way, we don't take time to think about whether being everywhere good or bad—or if what we're putting out there is any good. Mobile has tipped the scales on this as well. Your phone is always in your hand, at your desk, beside your bed. You check it 150 times a day, thinking that by checking it, checking in, and keeping in touch, you can somehow be everywhere at once.

The options for how to connect with an audience of potential customers grow every day—and exponentially more so with every new tool or site released to the market. There's this overwhelming pressure to feel that we've got to be using all these tools.

If you're one of the people who's guilty of trying to be everywhere and you don't know where to start—don't panic. I'm here to guide you through a few simple steps that will make a big difference for you and for your business—and ultimately, for your customers.

The biggest (and most easily solved!) problem here is that most people don't have a process for getting to good content and thinking of it from a customer-centric perspective. It doesn't matter how many new, exciting tools for connecting with customers pop up (I'm looking at you, social media). Bad content is still bad content.

The sticking point is that it becomes ten times worse if you're pushing content out through five different channels. When a customer visits a company's website and can see that the last time they posted anything on their site was two years ago, that customer will lose trust. What message does that send to customers? That the business owner isn't current. That they don't care. Has nothing happened at the company in two years?

Getting customer-centric content right, prioritizing it, and having a process for it has always been important. But now, because of the Internet, mobile, and social media, everything is amplified. You can't get away with ignoring your website anymore.

As a digital marketer who uses content as the bedrock to a great lead-generation system, I have developed a process to getting to the right content. I want to help you with that, too.

1. Educate.
2. Demonstrate thought leadership.
3. Generate leads.
4. Nurture leads.

Picture The ABC Company in your mind again, and imagine you're on their Facebook page. Which of those goals does that Facebook page fall into?

- Is it an education page?
- Is it thought leadership?
- Does it make you want to call them and do business with them?

For it to be education, there needs to valuable information. For it to be thought leadership, it needs to be something no one else is talking about or an angle that has not been considered. If you were to look at the content they've posted, and it is not clear which category it falls into, why would anyone follow their company page? And if what they sell means their customers are not using Facebook to find a product or service like theirs, then why are they there?

I can't tell you how many times I've talked to people who have this orphaned, horrible company page on LinkedIn or Facebook or Twitter. And when I ask them why it's there, they say, "We don't really know."

Another common problem is that many of the companies I encounter don't take the time to listen to their customers. There is an affliction among business owners that I like to refer to as "product goggles." This is when a business can only see the world through what they're selling as opposed to looking at the product's impact on a customer, the change it could make in his or her life, and what kinds of content they might need to help in that process. Then layered on to this "product goggles" issue is a lack of testing to see what works in marketing. They don't have a culture of testing to say, "Is this helpful? Is this useful?"

FOCUS ON PROBLEMS, NOT SOLUTIONS

Maybe anecdotally a salesperson will ask, "How'd you find out about us? When you were on our website, what were you reading?" But then the conversation stops there. That's a pity. We have all these tools now to measure these things. We can test and see these things at a really granular level—yet most companies aren't taking advantage of that. You wouldn't believe how many CEOs of small businesses can't answer the question "What does your Google Analytics tell you about your customers?" They usually say something like "I don't know. I don't go in there. The guy who manages our website looks after that." We'll cover this topic more in depth in chapter 2: Stop Guessing.

I go to a lot of meetings and meet a lot of CEOs, entrepreneurs, and business owners. The thing I hear from the people in charge most often is that they hate their website, because it doesn't "perform."

"So what do you want your website to do?" I ask.

"I want it to sell stuff."

"Okay, how would you set the website up in order to sell something?"

"We just want people to call us."

"Well why would they want to call you? What are you offering to them that helps them think that you're a company that they want to do business with? How are you presenting information?"

I walk it through. Then they sit back and say, "I get it—how do I fix it?"

There are a few simple steps they can use to get started. Sometimes they're willing to roll up their sleeves and do it, and other times they're not. In the following chapters, I will go into greater detail about these simple steps.

If you don't have a process in the first place, if you've got your "product goggles" on, then your expectations are unrealistic. Sometimes I'll be in a CEO peer group where everyone is complaining about how their salespeople aren't making enough phone calls, that they aren't generating enough leads and should be phoning more.

"Maybe we should try telemarketing," they say.

"How many of you take cold calls during the day from salespeople calling from other companies?" I ask. Not one CEO will put his or her hand up.

"Then why do you think there's a whole bunch of CEOs out there who want to take cold calls from *your* salespeople?"

This is what content marketing is all about. Let them come to you. Let them find you when they're doing research. If they can do a Google search and discover your well-optimized site, then they're getting to know you with the content you've posted. If you want to layer on outbound marketing and you need to follow up after somebody's left an email or phone number, then that's okay. You can gauge that based on your customer base.

There is this gap of understanding between using all of these tools as a way to sell and using them to listen and engage with your customers. When you just push out empty tweets, blog posts, or whatever—if your intent is simply to sell a product or service—you're going to lose people. It will come across as inauthentic, and your customers will disengage.

In the current landscape, there's a lot of guessing and a lot of old-school thinking about the way things work. I have a client right now who has nobody in marketing but has ten people in sales. The salespeople's responsibility is to go out and build relationships and talk to people on a regular basis. That's all cool, but when you're that heavily weighted in sales, it's hard to scale that when you haven't invested any time or money into your online strategy. At some point, even if a potential customer talks to a salesperson, the next thing he or she is going to do is go look up the company online.

The biggest problem right now is thinking that what you used to do offline will work exactly the same once it's moved online—that it is a direct translation from a brochure to a company website. Think about the example with the restaurant again. It might be cheap and fast for the restaurant to post a PDF of the menu online and say "good enough," but it's going to hurt them in the long run when people look them up online on their mobile phones and can't find what they need.

THE PROCESS IS BROKEN

What happens when people hire somebody to come and do marketing in their company? Oftentimes what gets taught in a university or college course about marketing and the science of putting a marketing plan together is not very useful or helpful. Marketing graduates may know how to do design, or how to do web development, but there isn't anything they can do that dives deeper into the marketing process or that goes beyond surface level. What is not getting taught in these courses is how to understand buyer behavior and why people make decisions to buy from one company over another, buy one product over another, buy one service over another. Without knowing that, what ends up happening is that marketing ends up being a big guessing game.

The problem in today's modern marketing world is that you have to be one part strategist, one part creative, and one part technologist—and then probably about five parts data analyst. You have to have all these different parts of your brain working at the same time. It's not just about coming in and being creative anymore. You need to understand how everything works together.

Most of the time, a company will hire somebody and think she will be able to just figure it out. They try to play the talent lottery. But more often than not, this new hire can't come up with a solution. The expectations about what that person is actually going to be able to do are just too high. And here's why: she doesn't have a process that is specifically based on the customer buyer path. She has been tasked with fixing the symptoms, when what she really needs to do is find the cure. Knowing what that cure is can only come from you: the business owner.

Too many companies are getting lost in a sea of options—but it's simply not possible to be everywhere and do it all well. Here's a quick overview of the advice I'll lay out in this book in greater detail. First, investigate how your customers buy products and services like the one you're selling. How do they go through their buyer journey to make the decision to buy? What role does each channel (your website, social media, etc.) fill? And what kinds of content can you create to engage customers? In the following chapters, I'll go into more detail about how, exactly, you can do this.

Once you've converted curious people into customers—they care. Then, you can test to see what the marketplace is thinking. You can test to see if your audience is ready to do anything about it. Once people have become customers, you need to think about ways to engage with them and keep them caring about the subject.

The expectation that social media or a company website is a direct portal to sign up for something is out of sync with where people are in the buying process. People who think this way don't have a good map or a good understanding for how people buy things and what matters to them in that journey. That's why the process is really broken today. It's a combination of not understanding the buying journey, hoping a new hire can just magically fix everything, and then executing a bunch of tactics that don't work, because they're misaligned with what's happening in the buyer journey versus the sales process. I'll debunk some more myths about social media in chapter 5.

EVIDENCE-BASED MARKETING

Discovering who buys from you is what I call the value proposition. Even companies that have been in business for decades struggle with this, because they've never been taken through a proper process to understand their differentiation in the marketplace. At Marketing CoPilot, this is a process that we take people through right at the beginning. What's your value proposition?

Who buys from you and why?[3]

That value proposition is then used to identify your buyer persona. Who is the buyer? What are the obstacles, proof points, or things that a person needs to know in order to make a decision to buy from you? Answering these questions will lead to a buyer map—the types of content they need from you, and what they want to understand about you before they engage with you.

Once you have that buyer map, you can create a content marketing plan coupled with constant online testing and data analysis. Eventually you can begin automating the process to mine data and understand that. We believe that this process is what many companies are *not* using today in the marketplace—and that this is where we think the companies have to start in order to really be able to do a good job of engaging their audiences. And the com-

---

3   A *value proposition* is the primary reason people buy from you. Some of the best research that has been done on this topic is by Dr. Flint McGlaughlin of MEC Labs. Here's a great example to help you understand the impact of value proposition and what it can do for your business. In the last 1970s, FedEx effectively branded itself as the fastest, most reliable shipping service with its tagline: "When it absolutely, positively has to be there overnight." That was competitive differentiation no other company could claim. At the time, the channel they chose to communicate through was simple and direct to their best customer. They didn't make a bunch of claims about their drivers or their trucks and try to figure out how to market to multiple audiences. They picked a differentiator and they stuck to living it every day in the business. And yes, competitors caught up, but they kept evolving. You can match competitors in many areas, but in one you have to excel. Once you identify where you excel, you'll know exactly what the theme of your content marketing should be and exactly where to be to tell that story.

panies that are doing it right? They're winning the game every time.

The businesses that are getting this right all have one thing in common: a really clear articulation of their value proposition. They're committed to the purpose of why their business exists and why people are buying from them. Take online Rx eyeglass retailer Warby Parker. They set out to make beautiful, well-designed glasses that didn't have to be expensive. But more than that, they wanted affordable designs available to all. So they layered in an element of social good with their business, creating a model where each time they sell a pair of glasses, they give a pair to people in need. It all circles back to their core value proposition: Everybody deserves good eyewear.

I have a client who sells some of the best caster wheel technology in the world. It may not be the most glamorous product, but their business does well because it's not just about the product. Their wheel technology may be amazing, but the reason that they've sold such good casters and have been committed to high-quality casters is because they want things to function properly. Whether it's for a hospital bed or a cart in a factory that moves smoothly so people don't hurt themselves, it's not the wheel they care about—it's the mobility. We've worked with them to really solidify that value proposition, and it resonates in the marketplace because it's not just about selling a product. It's about telling a story that matters. It's the experience, not the product.

ALWAYS BE TESTING

You can only win at this game once you get a real sense of why people care about what you do. In the film *Glengarry Glen Ross*, the famous line is "ABC—always be closing." But this is a dangerous game to play in marketing. In marketing, you should always be *testing*—ABT.

The reason there's so much bad content out there today and why people are struggling is because they are seeing the world through their product or service. They're having a very difficult time asking why their business or product matters to the customer. Once they can get into that mindset and really solidify the value proposition, it makes all the difference in the world. It's not an easy thing to do. You have to constantly work at it and you have to be constantly testing.

We've had clients who thought their value proposition was simple. They put it on a home page, and nobody clicked where they wanted them to click. Nobody downloaded what they wanted them to download. There would've been a time in the past when they would've looked at their marketing person and fired them. This is still a common reaction. But the real winners online realize that marketing is a constant series of tests. To develop a culture of testing means you have to have an assumption and willingness to sometimes get it wrong—and a plan to change it up when you do.

We have a client who was with us for three years, and during that time we must have done five different home pages until their message finally started to resonate. Now, funnily enough, they've backed up a bit and have done the work to think about the product as well. Because as they were testing, they wondered if maybe the product was too sophisticated, or if there were things they were focusing on in the product that the customers didn't care about. They've been able to use content as a way to evolve their value proposition and to evolve their product as well.

The sad truth is that many people don't want to take the time to do this. They think that it's time consuming, and they just want to get a new website or an email marketing campaign or the latest social media channel. But what they don't realize is that by taking the time to do this, the output is just so much better.

I'm willing to bet that your business already has all the raw components at your fingertips. You might not understand how to organize it, because you haven't stumbled on the tools to change the process. Maybe you have never done a customer scorecard.[4] You don't have a buyer persona or a buyer map. You haven't done a keyword strategy or any research to see what people are searching for. But I'm going to show you how to do all of that.

SOME GOOD NEWS

The fact that you've picked up this book is already a step in the right direction. In the following pages, I will illuminate a few simple steps you can easily take. It might not necessarily seem easier right out of the gate, but by paying attention to what matters to your customer, you can make your business better. You don't have to be everywhere. And trying to be everywhere is doing you more harm than good. But by keeping the customer in mind and creating a plan born out of common sense, you can make things better for yourself, your customers, and your business.

ABOUT THE AUTHOR

I've had more than thirty years experience in business, specifically sales and marketing. I now understand what a company needs to successfully connect with their customers, turn leads into sales, and stay competitive in a

4   For a customer scorecard, see http://www.marketingcopilot.com/customer-scorecard

rapidly changing marketplace. For you, it l starts here:
with this book.

I started my career in public relations, which was my first
foray into how to tell a story. Unfortunately, it was how
to *spin* a story. I leveraged what I was doing in the financial-services sector, taking complex topics and ideas and
trying to make them more consumable for people.

I didn't really get my hands dirty until I went to my first
software company as vice president of marketing and
had to put up one of their websites. It was nothing more
than our corporate brochure posted online. There was
no thought given to the sales process or what we were
really trying to accomplish or what kind of content was
usable other than features and functions. How little we
knew back then!

My world crossed over to online observance when I began
to write product sheets about software. We sold very complex systems to the financial-services industry that dealt
with fund order management and portfolio management
systems for brokers. We had raised a lot of money. We
were trying to build out what we were doing down on Wall
Street and we did a lot of selling in New York. Then it all
crashed in the early 2000s. It was one of those fire sales
that you heard about in the dot-com meltdown.

I started my own business, Marketing CoPilot, in 2003. Now I dedicate my time to helping business owners like you. We offer our proven methodology to any business or organization that wants to engage customers and prospects with content that starts the buyer journey. In the following pages, I'll share anecdotes of real businesses just like yours and show how our process delivers results again and again.

YOUR OPINION DOESN'T MATTER

• • • • •

When you talk to business owners as I do, you'll find that most will say they don't like their company's website and they don't think it's doing a good enough job. That's certainly been my experience running workshops. When I ask a crowd of people if they like their website, maybe two will put their hands up. But when I try to dig deeper and find out why, most can't get too specific. They'll complain that it's not performing, or that it doesn't accurately reflect their business, or that it's old or outdated or they simply just don't like it.

Over the years I've worked with many different software companies who build their home pages incorrectly. They think they're leading with their value proposition, but in reality it's just a list of all the features and benefits of their product.

Recently, I was talking to a manufacturing company who said, "The phone is not ringing." They were terrified that sales were going down. But when someone finally spoke to the receptionist about the phone not ringing, she informed them that they were getting flooded with emails asking for information about the product—and the senior management team didn't even know about it! For so long, they had been measuring the success of their digital strategy by call volume. This did not match reality.

A website should be an extension of your business strategy. But if you're struggling with your business strategy—about what to sell, who to sell it to, and how to sell it—then your website is going to be a mess. I know this with certainty because we've developed many websites for our own business, Marketing CoPilot, over the years. It has taken some trial and error to understand what we're selling and who we're selling to and what our ultimate expectations are for our website. Now, we've landed firmly in a place that we feel good about because we know it's backed up by facts. Our website has to be about thought leadership within the marketing space, because that's what our customers are looking for from us. But it's been an evolution.

It can be easy for a lot of companies to chase the lowest hanging fruit. They go after the customer and immediately try to make a sale, rather than offering the customer the information they need to solve a problem to build a relationship. Or, they base their strategy entirely on an opinion (and an uninformed opinion at that), or worse yet, a feeling about what they *think* should be on the home page. Believe it or not, discovering what should go on your website just takes a little digging.

In order to make your website resonate with customers, you need to examine what the customers think about you, your product, its value, and why they need it. If you can answer that for them and can continue to test that everything you're doing is working (and adjust when it's not), then you're headed in the right direction. But if you simply base your online strategy on a gut feeling, your website is never going to perform the way you want it to. After all, your opinion doesn't matter. But your customers' opinions do.

CUSTOMERS' UNDERSTANDING OF YOUR VALUE

A strategy based on opinion is not a strategy at all. But the truth is, you have to start somewhere. And for many business leaders, their opinion is the stepping-stone.

When an entrepreneur starts a new business, it begins very intuitively based on his or her individual personality. It's about what the entrepreneur thinks the brand should stand for, what he wants to call the business, and what's important to him. In the beginning, this is all coming directly from the entrepreneur. And while that may be okay in the beginning of a business, as the business starts to grow and evolve, he needs to examine things to make sure what they're doing reflects their customers' needs.

We've all encountered businesses and brands through-out our lives that give us the distinct feeling that we're dealing directly with the founder's personality—and not just their personality, but their opinion. I've witnessed it firsthand. These founders dictate the things they want on the home page (a drop-down menu with these specific options, a certain layout, the placement of a particular piece of information) simply because that's what they want, rather than digging in and looking at the data. In this way, they start making decisions and deciding to do things that could be completely counterintuitive to what their customers really want, simply because they're basing all their decisions on what they think has to be there.

A common problem is to say, "Let's put everything on the home page." People think everything the company does needs to be somewhere on the home page. They want to put it all there rather than think through what their customer needs in order to go through the process of making a decision to purchase.

I recently worked with a company during a value proposition workshop where we helped them develop a buyer map and keyword strategy, plus developed a very strong "wire frame" for their website. But when we put it in front of the CEO, he said he didn't want to do things that way. He said that he was about to go into the marketplace and raise money, and investors needed to hear certain things, and those certain things needed to be plastered all over the website. So instead of building a site for his customers, he built a site for potential investors. And then guess what? He was disappointed that his site wasn't performing in lead generation.

Another company hired us to go through this same process with them, and they were adamant that we do a home page test with five of their best customers to ensure that the value proposition was resonating. That was great because that CEO supported the idea that his own opinion doesn't matter. What mattered to him is the way his customers view their value.

There was a time in software marketing when it was all about a "free" trial. We thought that's what buyers wanted.

The thinking was that if we could just get people to sign up for a free trial, then they would follow through and buy it. This, as it turns out, wound up being a bad strategy. There was poor engagement with the product, and relatively few people took the next step to make the purchase. It was giving away the product without showing the customer what it could actually do. We gave it away and hoped the customer could figure it out.[5]

What we should have been doing was showing prospective customers the problems that the product could solve, then leading them to a controlled environment where they could test it, try it, and build a relationship with the product and the company. This kind of customer advocacy is important because it creates a stronger relationship with the customers and turns "trial-ers" into product advocates.

Subscription models and repeat customers are what build a business. In particular, subscription models help you create a situation where the customer is signing up to repeatedly receive and engage with your services on an ongoing basis. This is a great way to create a specific, mea-

....

5   In *The Inevitable*, Kevin Kelly suggests we will be newbies forever. The most important technologies that will dominate life thirty years from now have not yet been invented, so naturally you'll be a newbie to them. Unless you are prepared to start using a certain item "right now," a free trial for an item is just another thing on your to-do list that you're not ready for. You won't have time to learn something before it's replaced or before you go on to the next thing, so the point of a free trial is moot. If you really need it, you buy now.

surable value proposition because it creates a scenario in which a customer must continually make a decision about you, your business, and whether she likes what you're doing. And when she continually makes the choice to do business with you, it helps prove your value proposition over and over.

In our business, we sell a tested process and results. We want our clients' businesses to grow because they have their best sales tool—a strong digital foundation—to perform for their business. But to achieve this, you need data, not opinion.

The right way to get this is to develop a credible, specific, and measurable value proposition where you define who buys from you, why, and what attracts them to your company.

FOLLY OF RELYING ON OPINION IN PLACE OF PROCESS

Relying on opinion for designing your online presence is a lazy way of doing things, but I see it happen a lot. Most often at companies, the CEO makes all of the decisions simply because he or she is the boss. What the company should be doing instead is taking the time to actually understand the customers, their journey, and what they need from the company in order to make a purchase.

The mistake almost always starts at the top. The CEO will say that she wants the website to be a certain color, that it should have a particular layout, that the drop-down menus should be arranged just so. This is all based on her personal opinion of what she thinks should go where. This sea of conjecture is where the broken marketing strategy starts. As a result, many organizations miss the opportunity to create a process for developing and understanding their value proposition, defining their message, or getting specific about what their content and sales channels should be. In fact, a very small percentage of companies I've spent time with have a solid understanding of their value proposition and their best customer.

One of the most important things you can do for your business is to create a value proposition that outlines your buyer's journey and then regularly check in to make sure it's still holding up. Doing the work to get there can be a challenge. Although no one wants to be told that what he's doing isn't all that special—it's like telling someone his baby is ugly—if you're not getting the kind of results you desire, then it's really important to reevaluate.

I had one client who said to me, "This is such hard work. Can't you just go look at my competitor and copy what they did and put it on our site?" I said, "Yeah, I could. But then why should I buy it from you?" Because that's exactly what everybody on their website was going to ask if they seemed to be exactly the same as the competition. There was a time when companies used to be able to get away with that—to simply rip off of their competitors—but it doesn't fly anymore. Buyers know it. They can smell it. They can see that you didn't work hard enough to understand your unique selling proposition. And if you haven't done the work to tell your customers why you're special, they certainly won't do the work for you. Fewer than 5 percent of the more than 150 companies I've spent time with have a solid understanding of their value proposition and their best customer.

There is so much competition today in the marketplace, no matter what line of business you're in. Whether you sell flowers or dog food or computer software, there are millions of alternatives to solving a problem. Helping your customer choose you starts with a question. "Why should I buy it from you?" is the most important thing you can ask about your business, and it's the most important thing you can communicate to your customers. Because it's their opinion that matters—not yours. And it's your customers' view of your value that's going to drive your business forward.

Whether a business has one person in their company or 10,000, to be successful a business must have processes in place for different tasks. There is a process for accounting, a process for operations, a process for sales. Well, there should also be a process for marketing, too!

It's not just about measurement and making goals, but instead it needs to be about knowing the process and the specific steps necessary to achieve goals. Marketing and sales are very closely tied—and they just happen to be the two areas that companies tend to struggle with the most. This is because, often, there isn't a great process around sales: who you're selling to, how you're selling to them, how you're promoting engagement, how they'll go through the buying process, how to determine when a customer is ready to buy, and so on.

I often see companies that struggle with setting up this process, and the biggest problem they have is that they just don't have the information they need in order to figure out the questions they're trying to answer. But this is why a customer relationship management (CRM) tool is so important. A CRM tool is not a software product—it is a mind-set.

Here are the questions you should be asking yourself:

- How do we treat our customers and prospects?
- How do we bring them through the process?
- What are all the steps that we have to do to get them to a point of understanding whether or not we have the right solution for them?
- What are the same things that have to happen within marketing?

In the past, the process was different—simpler. It used to be easy to hire telemarketers, set up a direct mail campaign, or buy some ads in the paper. But that's not what the world looks like today. These days, things are much more integrated, and the funnel isn't so linear. The way a buyer looks for information and solutions today is very different than it used to be.

The Internet has blown up the conversation—and has had a major affect on the sales funnel. Now you have to be much more specific about who you want to reach and how you engage them.

It used to be that the business could control the conversation. Remember the film *Glengarry Glen Ross?* An army of salespeople could decide what the story was going to be. Because of things like social media, now it's the customers who are controlling the conversation. All they have to do is start a hashtag and suddenly they're dictating the conversation around a company or product—either good or bad—and the company doesn't have any control over it. All the company can do is react.

Without a strategy, you never know for sure what's working and what isn't. Not having a process for getting your customer through the sales funnel means that you're missing a valuable opportunity for connecting with them and for turning an inquisitive person into a customer handing over his money. A lot of companies just assume that a customer will come to their website and do the work of sifting through everything that's up there. The truth is: They won't.

Putting a specific strategy in place will help you serve up exactly what your customer wants in exactly the way she wants it. Only then is she going to pick up the phone and give you a call (or click and put something in her shopping cart, or hit a button and download the product). It's not the old days. You can't get away with simply putting an ad in the paper. The times have changed—and we need to change along with them.

You have to think about all the places that your best customer would look for information about you. That can be a lot of work without a process. When a business doesn't have measurable goals for something like a website, they put something together and then don't understand why it's not working. Instead, a process for website content needs to be an extension of your business strategy.

If you're struggling to articulate why you're the best at something and why people should buy that from you, then that's going to be reflected on your website and your social channels. If you don't have clear goals for what you want or for how you can solve a particular problem for your customer, then how can you expect them to buy from you? When you don't have goals, you can't measure success.

Many of the CEOs with whom I speak complain about hating their website, that it doesn't do anything for them. But when I ask for specifics, they can't articulate what they want other than to generate leads. If you want the main goal of your website to be about generating leads, then you need to know what kind of people are coming to your website and what they're looking for. And once they land there, what are they trying to do?

A website can do a lot of things and can have many varied goals. Here are the biggest and most important ones:

1. Educate a customer about what your business or product is all about.

2. Position your company as a thought leader within an industry.
3. Generate leads for the future.
4. Nurture the leads you've already made.

Small and medium-sized businesses tend to have this problem most frequently because they try to do too many things at once. If they are a new company or have a new product that requires a bit of explanation, then they may start out by trying to educate. But after time, things can evolve. They may need to shift gears into thought leadership, but their website is still in education mode. Now they're potentially losing people who are coming to them for thought leadership. Then after they transition their website into thought leadership, they need to set up a funnel on their website that will send people through a process that finishes with lead generation. Then once they have a pool of people who are interested—but not ready to make a purchase right now—they can start to nurture them.

This segmentation of goals is important, and it's something that a lot of companies make the mistake of not doing, or at least not doing well. Instead, they lump everything together. They try to educate and promote conversations and generate leads all at the same time. It's because they don't understand their customer and what their best customer wants from them.

"Okay, Marie, I get all that, but where do I start?" Start with the customer scorecard.

START WITH THE CUSTOMER AS YOUR AUTHORITY

Begin by making a list of everyone who has bought from you in the past year. If you're a start-up, it's a little trickier, but you can instead make a customer scorecard of the types of people you would want to buy from you. Visit Marketing CoPilot to get your own customer scorecard at http://www.marketingcopilot.com/customer-scorecard.

- What was it they were trying to accomplish that led to you as a solution for their unique needs?
- What are the emotional triggers you need to hit within them in order for them to make a purchase? For each of those customers, make note of the cost of sale and rate how hard it was for you to deliver your solution or product to them.
- Finally, make note of how the entire experience went. Would they refer you to a friend or colleague? Would they talk about your company in a positive way? When you put all of these things together, it will help you determine how profitable each customer was.

You can't be all things to all people, and you can't be everywhere—especially if you have committed time, money, and resources. But by determining who your best customers are and how you can reach them, it will maximize your efforts to model your entire process after those individual experiences. Therefore, start with your absolute best customer, look at his attributes, look at the vision of what he was trying to accomplish, and from there build out a value proposition and a content plan that will create that same experience over and over.

Too often as CEOs, business owners, and entrepreneurs we jump right to having an intellectual conversation about what we do. We're right into either the features and functions, or the facts and figures, or what we think are the benefit statements of what we do, but we haven't earned the right yet to have that conversation. We haven't yet hit on any emotional triggers that suggest we understand where the customers are coming from and their challenges. Until you hit that emotional trigger, you haven't earned the right for them to start clicking around your website, or reading your content, or following you on social media. Until what you're doing resonates with an audience, you won't have an audience at all.

When you have a customer score card, it allows you to understand what customers care about, thus enabling you to have a different (and better) kind of conversation that's based on emotional triggers, not figures and functions.

Knowing this will lead you to determining a buyer persona and a buyer map. And if you follow those closely, it will allow you to make better choices about how to present your business and your products online.

THE JOURNEY IS MORE IMPORTANT THAN THE DESTINATION

If you've picked up this book, it's because you're trying to use digital marketing in your business as a way to engage with your customers, meet prospects, and generate leads. Some of the old tools or techniques that we've used in the past aren't working anymore. There's too much competition. Customers today expect a very high level of transparency. They want honesty. They want helpful information and useful products. Over the last few years, content marketing has become one of the most powerful tools that businesses can use to engage prospects and nurture leads. It's a way to educate people and build thought leadership, and it will directly contribute to lead generation and lead nurturing.

Buyer behavior has changed forever, and there is no going back. The genie is out of the bottle. Now, we have to find a way to build a modern marketing program for our companies, and content marketing helps us do just that.

In the beginning of the chapter I mentioned how I often deal with software companies that build their websites incorrectly. They expect too much up front from the prospective customer. For one of these companies, the aha moment happened simply. They expected customers to enter their information right away. They thought that visitors to a website were ready to buy. So as a test, their CEO had someone call all the people who had submitted their information and ask them what they thought. What he discovered was that almost everyone had been annoyed by the phone call and were far from buying. Just because they had downloaded a piece of content didn't mean they were in cycle. This was important information. From here, we helped this client develop a content plan that would increase customer engagement and would help take the customer through a process, all of which was tracked and measured.

We were able to see all the places a customer visited on the website, how long she stayed, and which content she consumed. So by the time a customer hit the page with the brochure outlining software pricing, they could prompt the customer for her personal information.

And here's where the aha moment happened. The CEO didn't realize that there were so many steps involved before taking a customer to a place where he or she is ready "to talk." The truth is, all of those steps were happening before, but they were simply happening in a very different way with no visibility.[6]

At the end of the day, most people follow one of three categories after they've learned about you and have become interested on an emotional level:

- I either agree or don't agree, and I'm never going to buy from you and I'm gone.
- I agree with what you're saying, but I'm not ready to buy right now.
- I agree and I am ready to buy right now.

The epiphany that the CEO had about when a person might be ready to enter the sales process is a pretty common one. Maybe you need to have that aha moment, too. I've found that many business owners just don't realize that all of this activity is happening before someone is even ready to put himself on a list. That's the biggest opportunity available to you within digital marketing. When you have good content, it allows you to test.

6   Seth Godin has a great blog post that he wrote years ago about conversion rate. One percent is a conversion rate of anything. For pretty much anything you could think of, the conversion rate is 1 percent, unless you really know how to engineer it. Really, at the end of the day, you're not going to have a huge conversion point of a ton of people buying from you because you did content marketing. What you're going to have is people entering a stage that you can test and track over time.

→ Your opinion doesn't matter. It's your customers' opinion of your value that matters.

→ Understand who your best customer is by creating a customer scorecard.

→ To be considered, you need to have a modern marketing program based on the customer journey.

CHAPTER 2

STOP GUESSING

• • • • •

Marketing is one of those professions where people guess a lot. They think marketing is easy because it involves creative thinking. Unlike in accounting or operations, in marketing many people think they can contribute to the conversation, but often they contribute based on their own personal bias or opinion.

I've spent enough years in marketing—as director of communications, director of marketing, vice president of marketing, vice president of sales—to know that there are certain departments that are very quantifiable, where success directly correlates to numbers and revenue.

Marketing should be the same—it should start out with an assumption. Then goals and tactics should be set to prove that assumption true or false. Most companies fail to do this. They don't start with an objective in mind. They bring someone in to run the department, but that person is really just making things up as they go. I used to be one of those people who could go in as the marketing person and make things up. And I had some flexible, courageous, entrepreneurial bosses who let me spend time and money trying to figure it out. But through this I learned that there is a better way. We have to stop guessing. And that's actually what led me to build Marketing CoPilot.

I used to tell people they had "home-page-itis." They'd throw everything on the home page and hope that something stuck. They hoped that somebody would click somewhere. They didn't know how to figure out what should actually be there.

There has to be a process in place to determine the type of content that goes on your website, in your email newsletter, or through your social media channels. You're choosing to communicate with an audience, and you can't just take your product brochure and stick it online and think it's going to work.

There's been a huge, monumental shift in how we market today in terms of how the buyer does research before buying. Because of this, we're being forced to be much smarter about what kinds of content we choose to produce and which channels we choose to populate. One of the great things about marketing now versus a few years ago is that we have data available to us to help us make better decisions.

While marketing is still a bit of both science and art, it's the science part that we as marketers have to adopt more. We need to be a lot smarter about using data. We need to stop guessing. It all breaks down to a simple progression: map the buyer journey so you can decide what to do, then track how it's performing to decide what to do next. There's never been a better time as a marketer to rely on data as a way to tell us what can be improved.

I had a customer recently whose business log-in page for their customer portal was littered with social media icons. When I asked them how many people click on the icons as a way to communicate with them, share about them, or follow them, they didn't know. Then they changed their mind, called up the data, and said, "Very few." They didn't know how many people clicked from those icons to their home page. They didn't know how many of their actual customers followed them of Facebook. Their thinking was that having those icons made them look like they were in the game.

What we discovered was that they were failing miserably

with their social media strategy—in fact, there was no strategy! They had no traffic coming from Facebook to their website. Nobody was using the social media icons on their website to do anything with them. Nobody was following them as a result. They weren't using these accounts to communicate with their customer base, so there was no reason to follow them. Why would you?

We were able to look at the outbound and inbound data to the site to determine that, even though they were posting huge traffic numbers of volumes of people visiting their website, there was zero traffic and zero lift from their Facebook account. So one of two choices had to be made: either decide the objective of the Facebook account, or simply just get rid of it.

Not only were they doing the wrong things, but they were also not using their data. Because if after having those social media icons there for a month, three months, six months, not one person was using them to share, then those icons are just a distraction and they serve no purpose.

DATA IS EVERYWHERE TODAY

You have all this data available to you to help you make better decisions. There have been other instances when I have looked at clients' social media sites and we've been able to use Google Analytics to determine how well they are performing. You want to make sure you have a purpose for every tool you choose to use and that the tool is working.

You might discover that you are actually getting good traction in Twitter, that you're getting great prospects coming to your website or to your online store, and that customers are doing the things that you want them to do. Data is there to help you track that behavior and make decisions. As the chapter says, stop guessing; instead, use these research tools and data to think through the best opportunities for your business.

We had a client who posted five different value propositions on their website, with five different options for clicking through to more information. What we discovered after ninety days of testing was that people didn't pick of any them. None of the buttons were chosen. So our question was: Where *were* people clicking? And if they were not going anywhere, why? We looked at the following:

- Page drop-off rate
- Bounce rate
- Time spent on the page

What were they doing and why?

We went back to the client and helped them to create a tiered approach to how they displayed information about what they do. We started with these steps:

- We asked: "What's the first thing people think about when they think about software like yours? What do they want to know first?"
- We took them through the process of what it's like to be a potential customer of their business, putting them in the customers' shoes, and from there we mapped content and the process.
- Then we tested again over a ninety-day period.

After these steps, we adjusted the online marketing approach based on the results we received so that we could improve their conversion rates. There were many different inflection points that happened by being able to test and being purposeful with the data.

In today's modern market, we know that people don't want more choices—they want fewer. They are overwhelmed by too many choices, and they want to be led. The best-case scenario for customers is to land somewhere that resonates with them immediately, with a solution that can help them, and with a very clear path for taking the next step. They don't want to have sort through drop-down boxes and confusing navigation. They want simple, direct, and transparent information. Data helps us create that experience because it allows us to stop guessing at visitor behavior on a website.

It's been a common tactic for a while for a business to simply create a Facebook page because they think that they *need* to be there—that any business who wants to be taken seriously should have a Facebook page. We started seeing these Facebook icons popping up all over websites, or in commercials. How many times have you heard the words "Follow us on Facebook" at the end of a TV commercial?

The funny thing about our client with all the social media icons was that when we started to dig in and look at the data, we discovered that even though their traction via Facebook was terrible, they were getting a ton of interaction on LinkedIn. We advised them to start focusing their efforts there.

Figure out where the traffic is coming from and what kind of person is interacting with your business. Is it positive traffic? What are customers doing when they get to the site?

Since this client was getting good numbers on LinkedIn, then there must have been a very specific reason why. They needed to use their data to figure that out.

There are big companies today who have become phe-nomenally successful because they know how to mine and manipulate data. One company in particular is Amazon. They are geniuses at seeing and tracking exactly what people do. They invented the concept of "you may also like," by pointing customers to products similar to ones they've already bought or have already browsed. They give customers suggestions before they even realize they want something. And that's all based on data.

Amazon data scientists are able to look at search patterns across their site and know what people are searching for. They can know that if a person looks at *this*, then he may also look at *that*. It's all a very smart use of big data.

But small businesses don't need to be big data experts. In fact, what they need to know is at their fingertips. Most business owners I talk to feel as if their marketing isn't performing the way they'd like it to, and they're discour-aged. But they don't even realize they have all this great data available to them already.

The kind of data that you should be tracking is all based on how well your customers are engaging with you—how much time they spend with your content, how they find their way to your site, how often they return, and so on.

I looked at a site recently that had a bounce rate of 96 percent—meaning that for every one hundred people who came to the site, only four stayed. The other ninety-six immediately left. This begs the question: Why did they go there in the first place? And what was it about the site that led them to say when they got there, "Well, this isn't for me"?

Sometimes a high bounce rate can be good. If you're getting qualified leads on your site but you have a high bounce rate, then there may not be anything wrong with that. But what about those four people who stayed? There are a few things you should be asking yourself—and measuring—when it comes to how your audience interacts with your content.

- Where was the first click on your site?
- Why did people go there?
- Is it natural to click there first?
- While people were on your site, how many pages did they view?
- How long did they stay?
- Did they take any action, like subscribing to your newsletter?
- Did you offer an action to take, and was it taken?

There are a lot of things you can track to figure out the

answers to all of these questions. And once you know the answers, you can make decisions about what to adjust on your website. Then you can measure to see if your changes are working.

Another great piece of data that you should be looking at is referral traffic. This is actually a very powerful tool that many people overlook. Imagine you have a colleague who might be in a networking group and who keeps referring business to you. You'd want to build a relationship with that colleague, right? Well, the same thing is actually happening online. If you dig into the analytics for your website, you can see where your referral traffic is coming from—meaning which websites are linking to you and sending traffic your way. You should be getting to know those websites the same way you would get to know a person who keeps referring business to you.

Data can even help you decide what to remove or change on your website because you can track where people are going and what they're doing next. All of this data is available to you, virtually at your fingertips. The cheapest and most simple way to track data is via Google Analytics, but there are many other data sources that you can layer on top of that.

What I like to say to people, particularly people who are just starting to figure out how to keep track of their data, is that Google is the biggest player in this space. For any kind of online strategy today, it would be unwise to ignore Google—the reason being that they still have an unbelievable market share. They have become masters of big data and tracking, especially within their Google Analytics tool. They are constantly working to improve the way they track data. Some CEOs are doubtful of using Google Analytics because it's open source; some people are afraid to have that set of eyes on their data and would rather track it privately. That's why independent analytics tools were popular for a long time.

However, I have seen a shift away from this fear and have seen more and more companies gravitate to Google. The thinking now is that it will probably do more good than harm in the long run, and it's free—so why not play nice with Google? If you're a small business, then you want to start in the most basic way possible, and Google Analytics is where you need to start.

First of all, it doesn't cost you anything (unless you feel there's a high price to sharing the information on your site.) Once you paste the code, Google has access to what's going on within your website, which to a certain extent you want anyway if you hope to get ranked well within search. And because Google is the biggest player in the search game, it helps to know what they're using to determine how well your site will rank.

There are two sides to it. It tells you something about what's happening on your site, and the data within it is telling you what you should be paying attention to as you're trying to improve your own search results. So until someone comes along to knock Google off their pedestal, you can't ignore them.

And while Google Analytics is relatively easy to learn and use, it's also important to educate yourself on what's going on. I think it takes a trained eye to understand what you're looking for and how to interpret the data. Quite frankly, data unto itself is useless. There needs to be analysis next to it.

So many companies dismiss all this information that's available to them. They say they never look at it, and that it's confusing or hard to use. But I'm here to tell you it's not—so stop making excuses!

We create thirty-day reports for all of our clients. Originally we tried to standardize it—here's the kind of information you should be looking at, this is how you want to slice and dice the information, this is what matters as far as results—and without fail every single CEO and vice president of sales we worked with wanted to display the information differently. So we came to the conclusion that because they all have different business objectives and they're all trying to achieve different things, they want to mine different types of data to support a different assumption or hypothesis. So we couldn't just do a standardized report; every client needed a customized set of data.

Google has some great tutorials and ways for you to learn about Google Analytics, what it does, how it works, and what you can look at. The real trick, though, is applying it to a business scenario.

You need to use analytics as a way to measure whether or not something you're doing is working. Set a goal, and then use the data to see if you've met that goal. If so, great. Do more of it! If not, ask yourself what you can adjust. That's the trained eye that many people don't have within their company.

The reason marketing is so challenging today is that you have to be a strategist, a technician, a data analyzer, and a creative all at the same time. To run marketing in a small business these days is no small feat. You might be well-versed in one area, but not so much in another. That's why

Google Analytics is so useful—it's easy to learn right out of the gate, and you can apply it to your business.

CONTEXT AND INSIGHT

The challenge with digital marketing and online strategy today is that, unlike marketing in the past—when you went to a trade show and met people, or you went out networking, or you used telemarketing—is that now there's a browser and a screen that separates you from a potential customer. This makes it harder to know a person's true intentions and to understand their buying journey. It's tough because you can't look someone in the eye anymore while they learn about you. You don't get to ask them questions. What you're trying to do is use well-placed content to understand them and guide them. When you use data to track their intentions, you get a better understanding of what works and what does not.

Whether a visitor to your page is doing preliminary research to learn what your business is all about, or if she's just shopping around and seeing what her options are, your content can serve as a resource. Even if she is just trying to educate herself about what you do while figuring out her options, you can use the data from her interactions on your site as a way to understand your customers' buyer journeys.

If you believe that you need to be a thought leader in your industry as a way to get the word out about a new idea or a new concept that you're trying to promote, and you're creating content around your ideas but realize nobody's downloading or reading that content, you're not going to get very far as a thought leader, because your efforts are not getting shared. This is where the data comes in. If you can take a hard look at what the numbers are saying behind the scenes, then you can adjust your strategy accordingly and get better at achieving those goals.

We had one business client not too long ago who was great at honing their content strategy. They were doing a lot of great blogging, posting twice a month on topics that had come directly from their field, but they weren't always getting great traction on their posts right away. The interesting thing with them is that they started to receive questions during sales calls that were directly related to something they had posted on their site—but from a few months back.

People were coming to their site and interacting with their content that was a few months old, but it was prompting them to ask specific questions. These blog posts positioned them as a thought leader within this space and were allowing their customers to ask all the right kinds of questions. This kept an open conversation going between the business and their customer base until the customers were ready to buy. That's the best kind of data and the best kind of content—when it keeps a conversation going and reminds people that when they're ready to come back and talk to you, you will be there.

What the inverse can tell you is just as useful. When you have a popular blog post that people keep coming back to, it can help you determine the types of content that people find valuable. When you have content that people keep returning to over a period of time, it establishes you as a resource for information.

For example, while working with a client of ours—a financial advisor—to develop a blog strategy, we helped him discover how his unique voice and expertise was what kept his audience engaged and coming back for more. He had done a piece illuminating why Warren Buffet's bond strategy wasn't a great strategy for the average investor. After he posted this, we saw great traffic and traction—especially among financial pundits on social media, who identified this as valuable information to share—which drove downloads to a white paper he had written about his own personal investment philosophy. What this told us was that the average investor didn't have a great grasp of bonds and was trying to learn more about them and understand how they worked. Because our client provided resources on this topic, people kept flocking to it. Now that he learned this through his site data, he could continue creating content that spoke to his core audience, while staying true to the value proposition of his personal brand.

> **What are "vanity metrics" and why should you be beware of them?**
>
> Sometimes, the numbers don't tell the whole story. Take Instagram for example. If you run a cheap contest or challenge within your Instagram caption—tag a friend who would like this photo!—that results in a lot of likes but no conversions. That's a vanity metric. That high number of likes may make it look as if you are getting a lot of interaction with your audience, but it's empty and just for show.

KEYWORDS—THE FOUNDATION OF YOUR DIGITAL ENGINE

Knowing and understanding what people are searching for online can be a great way to inform your content strategy. Regardless of what you're doing, a well-researched keyword strategy will serve you well. At Marketing CoPilot, when we work with clients to develop their keyword strategy, we begin with buyer personas.

⊙ What kind of customers are they trying to attract?

- What are these customers' priorities?
- What problem are these customers trying to solve?
- What are these customers trying to accomplish?
- What are some of the reasons why these customers wouldn't choose you?

After we take our clients through that, we are able to brainstorm a slew of keywords that people may be using, and then we work backward to develop content that supports those keywords.

This is the best way to engineer a keyword strategy as opposed to what a lot of companies do, which is simply to post a list of their products and services. We did a project for a large telecommunications company in Canada, where we are based, who has a very fragmented marketing strategy since what they sell varies from region to region. When you enter their website, the first thing you see is a prompt asking where you are.

So this company came to us for some strategy help. They were spending millions on Google Adwords and were not sure if the strategy was on the mark. We asked them what they thought their most popular keyword should be, the word they thought would be the best to start building content around, and their answer was "iPhone." But everyone online is trying to use the word iPhone. It's a popular search term! So we explained that it was going to be difficult for them to rank on the first page of Google based off the search term "iPhone." There's just too much competition. Plus, is that even what they should be trying to rank for in the first place?

When we looked at their buyer persona in the small business space, we discovered that their ideal customer wasn't even searching for information about iPhones. Instead, they were searching for very specific solutions to the kind of communications challenges that small business owners face.

After doing research for them, we discovered that their most powerful keyword was around "switching carriers." Now here was a topic they could dive into from a content perspective. Everyone needs a phone to do business, and as these small businesses grow, their needs change and they go searching for better communications solutions. It was a great topic for them to build excellent content around.

They started to build their site with content built around this topic. Consequently, they saw some great results. Since they could see via their buyer personas what mattered to their customers, what their priorities were, and what they were trying to accomplish, they saw better engagement and better lead generation—and it was all done through keyword research and a proper keyword strategy.

Even though putting together a keyword strategy can be tricky, at the end of the day, looking for opportunities to attract your ideal customer is going to provide you with huge returns. It helps to have someone who knows exactly what he or she is doing. (Remember: Stop guessing!) It might make sense to hire somebody to help you dig in and discover the twenty words you should be trying to rank for in your copy, because that's going to drive the right kind of traffic.

EMAIL MARKETING IS NOT DEAD!

Many tech pundits talk about the death of email marketing. They believe that other types of tools such as social media are taking over in how buyers want to consume information and interact with companies. Yet, in the 2015 Digital Marketing Survey we conducted of buyers and sellers of products and services, over 70 percent indicated they still prefer to interact and receive information from a company via email (versus 1.2 percent by phone).[7]

....

7   Download the digital marketing survey at:
     marketingcopilot.com/2015-digital-marketing-survey

Sending out a newsletter via email is one of my favorite ways to understand audience engagement and mine data. There are many ways you can use it to test things, which we often do for clients. Not too long ago we did a test with a client who was sending out safety guides. We tried to figure out if the information was better suited for senior managers or for safety supervisors who worked on the shop floor. The sales department of this company thought that safety managers were going to love these guides. However, we believed they would think they already knew what was in the guide and this content was better suited to senior managers who had safety as a part of their jobs but not as their main focus. Ultimately, the people we actually wanted to connect with were the senior managers, since they were the ones making the buying decisions.

We tested this by sending out an email campaign that had two columns: one with copy for the safety managers and one with copy for the senior managers. Both columns led to the same download. This allowed us to test who was downloading the material the most. What we found in the data was that the open rate was a lot higher for the safety managers. Since safety is their number-one priority, the headline appealed. But then as soon as they clicked through, they bounced. They knew it already. However, within the second column, the one aimed at the senior managers, there was a higher conversion rate because they were looking at the big picture for the company and trying to find new ways to do things.

The reason I love data in email marketing is because it allows you to test things in a way that can help you understand where you should direct your content. Within seventy-two hours of sending out an email, you can get some pretty good stats simply by using a proper email marketing tool.

My best advice is to start small with simple tools that are easy to understand. Then as you get better at it, as you become more invested with your strategy and spend more time on content, you learn about what drives engagement, and then you can upgrade to more sophisticated tools. And when you get good, you can get even better data to drive your business results.

Let's say I'm trying to snag a deal with a big company like Coca Cola. With some sophisticated tools, I could use the Coca Cola IP address and figure out how many times people from the company have come to my website, how many pages they viewed, and what they looked at. It may make me sound a bit like a stalker, but it's about becoming better at doing your research. That way when you do pick up the phone to chat with someone at Coke, you're already informed about the things that are important to him or her.

Knowledge is power. The kind of information you can glean from understanding your analytics is the difference between a cold call that goes nowhere and an engaging presentation that ends with a sale. It's all about how you're using information to support having a better conversation with a potential or existing customer.

CONCLUSION

In the end, our friends with the Facebook icon on their home page decided that it was important for them to remain on Facebook but that they would invest in being more thoughtful about the type of content they were posting. And they rethought the placement of the icon, opting to put it in the footer of their site rather than somewhere where the customer would just ignore it. It might end up that it's useful for a very specific subset of their customer base.

You have to stop thinking that whatever you choose to do online is a once and done scenario. There seems to be this hangover from the late 2000s that suggests simply having a website is all you need—that you put it up and that's good enough. You don't ever have to go back and change anything. We always tell people, "You wouldn't hire an employee and then not talk to him for a year. Why are you doing the same thing with your website?" Not understanding what's going on behind the scenes with your web analytics is like not talking to your employee. You have to manage your website the way you would a member of your staff.

It could be that it's still hard for business owners to wrap their heads around the skill set required to understand their web analytics. But when I talk about having a Facebook icon on the log-in page and not one person can tell me why it's there and what it's doing for them, I have to stop and wonder what else they aren't paying attention to within their web presence.

You can't just put something up on your site, expect it to do its job, and then walk away. We come across this all the time—these abandoned tools and products littered all over a site that people don't quite know what to do with. I asked a company about their social media pages—why they have them, why they don't update them, and so on—and they answered that it was the intern from a few summers ago who set it up, and then they left and took the password with them, and no one can figure out how to get back in there. We've seen this issue on a much bigger (and frankly scarier) scale when a company's domain name is up for renewal and no one knows where the URL was originally purchased or how to renew it. If your website went down for two weeks, would that be a problem for your business?

I'm willing to bet the answer is *yes*.

The crucial point here is that you can't just set it and forget it anymore. Everything needs to evolve continually.

Companies for which we consult work in increments of ninety days. Rather than setting up a hard and fast plan for the whole year, they work in three-month intervals where they look to see what's happening, and then they adjust. If one email template isn't working, they switch it up and use another. If one landing page isn't working, they make some changes and see if they can get better conversion on another. A modern marketing program has to be based on the assumption that it's a series of tests. You're always going to iterate, and it's a process of monitoring, assessing, adjusting.

And because we have data available to us, we can actually be doing this every thirty days. The information is available to us like it's never been before. It's all about deciding a reasonable test period and then monitoring, testing, monitoring again, and evolving. For most businesses I would say twenty months is way too long, and daily is just too fast. When you start to get fixated on the data within a day-to-day basis, it can actually work against you. You need to have a bit of distance to make sure there's a vision for mapping where you are to where you want to go.

You don't need to be everywhere. You just need to be in front of the people who care in a relevant and consistent way. And rather than adding on all these bells and whistles, every new social media channel that becomes available to you, if you took a popular blog post and spent time on five different ways to say that same thing, then it's a much better use of your time. Inherent in every web analytics tool is data that suggests where you should be spending your time. We can't be everywhere in this day and age. It's impossible. So go spend your time in the places that you're going to have the biggest impact as a business. And if nobody's on your Facebook account, then why are you there?

➥ There are great tools available to you for tracking data. Make them your friends.

➥ Use tools to test what's working for you, and then build off what is performing well.

➥ Don't get caught up in the hype of high numbers—focus on how they apply to your specific sales funnel and stop guessing.

CHAPTER 3

GOOD ENOUGH VERSUS GOOD

"What should we do with our website?" A company came to me recently with this very specific, very common problem. This company deals with information technology (IT) system integration and helps other businesses implement software products into their operations. They were suffering from a common issue: They expected too much information from their customers right up front. They had grown up in the click-to-buy way of thinking, where they expected someone to come to their website and immediately take action to do business with them. "We've spent $100,000 on our website, and when people visit, they don't pick up the phone and call us," they told me.

So I took them through the process of developing content to engage their audience and walked them through the steps of how to build an online presence that will engage and entice. But they weren't having any of it. They decided that since they had already spent all this money to redo the website, they weren't going to spend any more, and they didn't care if it didn't perform. They were happy with having a website that was "good enough," but were missing a major opportunity to go after something that was truly good—or possibly even great.

There is content out there (websites, newsletters, whatever) that companies constantly push to their audience without any process to back it up. People think they can just throw a newsletter together with what they—the company—think is interesting, when instead they should be building content around a framework dedicated to understanding what their customers care about.

Let's go back to that IT company for a minute. While digging around their website, I discovered blog posts about the company picnic they had just held. Here's how my conversation with them went:

"Who is this blog post for and why did you post it?" I asked.

"Well, we were told by an SEO company that we should

be constantly posting new content."

"Do you think your customers care about your company picnic or are searching for it?"

"Probably not..."

The content was out of line with the service they offer. It made no sense to have it on the site. It was jarring. And the problems continued when I took a look at their newsletter.

REMEMBER THE 1960S JAPY SCRIPT TYPEWRITER?

This is a problem I see a lot. People don't know what content to create, so they take a template and try to fill it with whatever they can think of instead of taking the time to go through their goals for a particular piece of content.

Rather than posting about the company picnic, you need to be asking questions like these: "Who is this newsletter for? What do we want them to know, feel, or do as a result of receiving it? What kind of engagement do we expect to get by sending something out?"

The primary purpose for an email marketing campaign is to create an action. Maybe it's a click-through to a website, but you want a measurable action that leads to a next step.

Once you have them interested, the goal is to get them to take action—most often by clicking through to your company's website. Unfortunately, most people still think email marketing is simply to sell something.

WHY GOOD ENOUGH DOESN'T CUT IT

Content that matters internally is not the kind of content you want people to be focusing on in the marketplace. A story about your company picnic does nothing for your customer. When you create an email marketing message or newsletter—whether it's industry news or content that educates—you can't just guess. You need to do the work to figure out what customers care about and then serve that. As we covered in the last chapter, "Stop Guessing," it all starts with tracking data and building off of what is working. Once you do the research and use tools that are at your disposal, suddenly you have this great opportunity to have a customer conversation that no one else is having. But now that you know the content on your site needs to change, how do you change it? And what constitutes good content? We'll cover all that and more in this chapter.

Here's something I've heard from people when I ask how their links are performing in their email newsletters: "We really don't know. We're just pushing stuff out and hoping that it does something." Sound familiar? So many of us are guilty of this at some point. We think that the most important thing is to just get something out there into the universe, anything to show that we have a presence online. But have you ever stopped to think you may be doing more work than you need to?

When you take a step back to investigate who your content is for, how you'd like them to feel as a result of receiving it, and what you want that person to know, you begin to create a framework that serves your customer rather than you—and that's a good thing. Once you've established what your goals are, you need to make sure you're tracking performance to see if what you're doing is working. Measuring results helps you to pivot if necessary, reinforce what's going well, and determine where to go next.

Remember the story about the company picnic on the company blog? Even though they thought they were doing the right thing by putting it on their site, it wasn't working. And if you're guilty of this, too, I can tell you it isn't working for you either. That content is about you, not about your customer. And that's a major misstep. Until you fix those components and begin to think about your buyer's journey, your web strategy isn't going to work, and your website isn't going to be able to perform as a lead-generation tool. Simply throwing something on your site, shrugging your shoulders, and settling for "good enough" doesn't cut it anymore.

Companies try to use content to be everywhere. They think that if they post something, stick it in their monthly newsletter, share a photo on social media, and simply get it out through as many channels as possible, then people will pay attention because content is content, right? Well it's not. They may be meeting the criteria of the activity, but they're missing the other half: what the customer wants. These companies think that just putting up some content that they believe is "dynamic" will help with their dynamic search ranking.

When Google crawls a website, it sees two types of content. The first is content that's been sitting there for a while, like the About Us section, the Products and Services page, or a company's contact information. This is identified as static content. However, if you have a blog or a newsletter or something that is frequently updated and time sensitive, this is seen as dynamic content. Because dynamic content is by nature new and fresh, it indexes higher on Google.

This causes a problem. People have caught on to what makes a page rank higher in Google, and they've tried to hack the system. They think the only thing that matters is to update their page with something new and fresh—so they focus more on the quantity of posts rather than on the quality. This is how you wind up with a post about the company picnic on the blog; someone is simply trying to meet their update quota for the week. But what they're missing are the tools they need to properly create the right content—content that's good rather than just good enough.

Good enough doesn't cut it because there's too much competition. The possibility to be overlooked is instantaneous. When you're a smaller organization and you're fighting for eyeballs, good enough just doesn't work.

You need to focus first on getting the basics right—your site, your content—before you try to be anywhere else. You can't be everywhere, remember, and you shouldn't try to be. It's more important to be in a few places and be good than to be everywhere and just be good enough. I would even argue that you're better off doing nothing than settling for something that is simply "good enough" for your customers.

TRULY GOOD

Instead of trying to do everything and be everywhere, being truly good means going back to the basics and focusing your efforts on what makes you—and your company—special, different, and important versus alternatives and competitors. Content that is truly good starts with developing a value proposition spectrum that spans your business, from your company's overall purpose to the problem you solve for your customer.

Defined value is what builds a brand and ultimately leads to a sale. Compelling and clearly stated values move a person quickly from doing research to becoming a customer. A value proposition is the primary reason somebody buys from you, and this is what most companies struggle to articulate in a compelling way. These companies think what's most important about them is what they do, that it's all about the features and functions. But in fact, what's most important is what a company's *customer* finds important.

The spectrum upon which a value proposition is composed is multifaceted, diverse, and complex, but what many people don't realize is that by not having a compelling value proposition, they're not giving their customers a reason to interact or engage.

Say you send out an email to your customers. The first step is to determine how you're going to get people to open your email. One way to try to answer this question is to start with the inverse. What are some of the reasons why people may *not* open it? Maybe they don't recognize the sender, or the subject line doesn't resonate with them, or they don't think the email applies to them. You want to be seen as a trusted source—regardless of the topic.

Once they've opened your email, now what? You want them to read it, engage with the content, and take the next step that drives them to your site, your content, or your products. How do you get them to do that? That next step needs to feel natural and draw them in easily via great content.

Many companies either don't think this through or skip it altogether. They don't do the work that's needed to determine their value proposition. You should always be asking yourself these two questions:

- Why would somebody want to hear from me on this topic or about this product or service?
- What is the value (in the customers' eyes) that only I can bring to the table?

The second step is all about the buyer persona and figuring out what is most important to your customer. If you skip this step and continue to create content anyway, all you're really doing is throwing things at the wall to see what sticks. But when you determine your buyer persona, you create a strategy where, more often than not, the content you make is going stick.

We recently worked on a buyer persona[8] for a group of distributors in Canada who deal with safety products (think: goggles, gloves, helmets, vests, etc.) and who had worked with a cooperative to create a private label brand of products. So we needed to figure out what the buyer journey looked like for their customers and what needed to happen in order for someone to make a purchase. Ultimately what it came down to as the most important thing to a potential buyer of this product was whether or not this company's product was superior to the product the buyer already used.

Let's take a step back and go through the buyer journey. There's a construction worker (let's call him Bob) who wears work gloves every day on the site, but the gloves his company gave him and everyone else he works with just aren't cutting it. His company is looking into upgrading their standard-issue work gloves, but because they need to buy upward of 1,000 pairs, they're keen on getting a good price and making sure the cost-effectiveness of their new gloves makes sense. They want the best quality for the best price. So with this all in mind, they set out looking for a new pair of gloves.

8   According to Adele Revella of the Buyer Persona Institute and author of the book *Buyer Personas*, a buyer persona is built from interviews with real buyers. It tells you what prospective customers are thinking and doing as they weigh their options. The buyers' words reveal the attitudes, concerns, and decision criteria you need to address to win their business. At Marketing CoPilot we start with the buyer personas and map the buyer journey so that we can create a topic that speaks directly to what a customer needs to know when looking for a product or service. To learn more, visit http://www.buyerpersona.com/buyer-persona-template.

While doing their glove research, they come across a new private label product. They're intrigued, but they're unfamiliar with the company who makes them—this lack of brand identity is a potential barrier to purchase—and they're not sure if they can trust them. Other reasons why they may not make a purchase include availability of the product, where it's made, and of course the price.

After a bit of research, Bob determines that the new gloves are matching up with their criteria—it's a better quality product at better value. So what happens now? Because these gloves aren't available in stores, they're going to ask for a sample by reaching out to the company that supplies them. So they reach out to a distributor and get a quote. At this point, they're going to be comparing products, visiting company websites to see how competing products stack up, and reading testimonials and reviews of the product. Once they feel that they have all the information they need and they've settled on the best option for their employees, then they're ready to make a purchase. This is the important first step in the buyer journey. Interestingly, the supplier of the gloves has not heard from them yet and doesn't know they exist and are looking. This is likely happening right this minute with your own business.

This was a huge epiphany for the guys selling the safety gear. When they first brought us in, it was simply because they wanted help with their website. But after we started asking questions, we determined that the reason why people would go to a website is to ask for a sample. This was not what they originally thought the website would be used for. The truth was, no one even knew that these new products existed, and they were going to have to go through a distributor to get more information about pricing before they could buy anyway.

By going through this process and identifying their buying persona, we identified the first thing a customer would do is to ask for a sample. Now, knowing this, the website can become a useful tool. At this point their customers have heard the name, so they go online and see the product they're interested in and write a message on the contact form that goes straight to the distributor. This gives the distributor the opportunity to now deliver what they need—the sample—and hopefully, close the deal. This offer becomes more powerful than paying for product-centric AdWords.

When Warby Parker first started, people said, "You'll never be able to sell eyeglasses online because everybody wants to try the frames on." But they were smart. They sent out up to three pairs of glasses to anybody who went online and asked for them. If you kept a pair, then you paid for them. If you didn't like them, you just sent them back.

This was brilliant. Even if you, the customer, are not ready to buy, Warby Parker still finds a way to engage with you and with your unique criteria in mind.

This type of strategy is powerful because it serves the customer. It was a strategic decision to implement this type of "try before you buy" solution, but it creates much higher customer engagement than buying ads on Facebook or some other social media tool.

Perceived barriers are things that Warby Parker discovered early in their business design. You start by asking yourself, "Why wouldn't my ideal customer (people who like fashionable frames but don't want the same old thing or to spend a fortune) buy from us?"

Make a list of the same things for your business. Why doesn't your ideal customer buy from you? Is it because of your return policy or guarantee? Is it your delivery of the product or service? Is it because they need to touch or feel something first before they commit? All of these reasons will lead you to create conversions points you can test against. For example, if customers need to touch or feel something, send them a sample and build the cost to do this into the sale. At the very least, you have someone committed to giving you her contact information—and with the right nurturing campaign, you can get to know her until she are ready to buy. Perceived barriers become your best marketing tools.

You could build a website with all your products on it and spend $2,000 a month on AdWords so that you can drive traffic to the site, but it would do nothing for your company from a sales or a lead-generation perspective. Taking people through the buyer journey process shifts the paradigm. Taking the time to do this work is how you become good instead of being good enough.

There's a nonprofit I've been working with, Kids Now, which runs after-school programs for kids in grades seven and eight to build self-confidence and self-esteem before they transition into high school. It's a great program that helps kids at a critical time in their personal development. We've been helping them with their online strategy, which was all over the place. There were drop-down boxes everywhere, way too many places to click, and things were just oddly placed. If you wanted to donate to their cause, you had to make too many clicks in on the site. It was not a great setup for a nonprofit that relies on donations!

This is an example of a website with no compelling value proposition, no clearly identified buyer map, and no clearly identified objective. They were putting everything they could on the home page without realizing how confusing it was for people. I pointed this out to them, and they said, "Oh my God, you're right. We built this website four years ago, and we've just kept adding more stuff to the home page hoping that somebody is going to click on something."

They told me the primary goal for their website is to raise money via corporate (not individual) donations. So I suggested their website needed to be about educating on the problems and how that fit into corporate agendas. We walked through that strategy together. They don't have deep pockets to go after an individual donor strategy, but they realized they have huge success by going after corporate donations. Knowing this, we have been able to tailor the website to this.

"Well, what about the kids?" they asked. As I pointed out, kids aren't really using their website—a place like Twitter is better equipped to be the communication point for kids because that's where they are.

This is the idea of focus. When I say focus, I mean focus on your primary objective. You can't be all things to all people. You have to make choices, and that's what leads you to good. You need to make choices and narrow your focus, taking away everything superfluous until you've tested to see whether people have bought into your value proposition.

It's hard to make these kinds of choices and keep an overall goal in mind. You probably have limited time, money, and resources, and you may be having a hard time right now struggling to see the forest through the trees. You're actually going to feel better when you've made those choices because things are going to be simpler to get out the door. At the end of the day, if your content isn't helping your customer, then it isn't helping you.

MORE WITH LESS

You are going to have to dedicate some funds and resources to your new strategy, but ultimately you will see a lot more proverbial bang for your buck. What's important is focusing on where you're going to have your best wins.

I find it disconcerting when a company expects to hit big numbers (either in sales or in revenue) without being realistic about building the relationships they need in order to get them there. The nonprofit we worked with came to us after they had done a social media campaign. They thought it would help them get more donations. They had run a campaign asking people to post photos using a specific hashtag, and they got a ton of impressions. But they didn't raise a dime. And they didn't get any new corporate sponsors through the initiative, proving it was fun for kids but not for the donors.

When you look at Avinash Kaushik's model of See-Think-Do-Care, this social media campaign falls squarely in the See phase. People always think social media campaigns are going to drive lots of traffic or sales, but the truth is, that's not how social media works. These channels can be good for driving awareness, for sending a person to your site for more information, and hopefully for that person taking another action. As it turns out, lots of people went to the Kids Now home page via the campaign, but the home page didn't engage and have people take a next step.

In fact, you actually had to search around a little bit and click through to a few places before you could donate. They may have generated all this visibility, but they didn't make it easy for someone to take the action he or she wanted because the company didn't understand what it felt like to visit the website for the first time. Once we walked them through the buyer strategy, it hit them: This social media campaign didn't actually work, despite all the impressions they received.

Avinash Kaushik's See-Think-Do-Care Model

SEE—The largest addressable, qualified audience. (This is where social media may come into play in your business, as a place where people see you but are not ready to buy. You also need to test to see if the right people are seeing you.)

THINK—The largest addressable, qualified audience with some commercial intent. (This is where you need a conversion point to determine just where they are in the buyer journey and if they care about your specific value proposition.)

DO—Largest addressable, qualified audience with lots of commercial intent. (This is where you are testing to see if they want to go to the bother of getting a sample, signing up for something with detailed information, etc. Did they just share on Facebook or did they actually donate?)

CARE—Current customers with two or more commercial transactions. (This is where they do more than donate once because they liked the ice bucket challenge. This is when they feel passionately about your cause. There is a difference, and long-term businesses are built on people who care, not just people who buy once.)

Elevating your content strategy isn't about becoming a better writer or coming up with fancier or funnier copy. When you elevate your content strategy, you're thinking through what's happening with that content when a user is consuming it and getting to know you. To do that well means continually testing and continually iterating. That's where the time, money, and resources come into it. If you think you'll just build it out and leave it undisturbed for the next six months, then it's not going to add any value. Instead you have to start thinking of it as iteration with continual testing and reinvesting.

Had the CEO in the newsletter example followed our process, he could have collected a series of twelve problems that he saw happening with customers after they'd bought from him and set out to solve and write about those problems.

Here's a great example of one of those potential problems: We've just implemented a CRM system, but nobody in the company is using it. What do we do now? Or another problem might be this: We can't get easier adoption because people aren't entering the right data, what do we do now? Had the CEO sat down each month and written an article answering these kinds of questions—the questions that matter to his customers—emailed them out via the newsletter, and then driven them back to a well-structured website that provided more resources on what he was talking about, then that would have been a huge win.

All this time, money, and energy is getting spent when a better win would have been to sit down and identify twelve important problems that were solved by the company and once a month be sending those out with an identified conversion point.

Instead, they've got a marketing manager reacting to internal suggestions, with no process in place, coming up with stories about the company picnic. The CEO is spending all that money on a salary and it's being wasted. When there's no identified process and no compelling value proposition or buyer persona, there's no way to create a framework for compelling content. So time, money and energy gets wasted. It would be better to sit down and identity the ten to twelve most important problems the customer has and how the company/product/service can solve them.

When you spend the time to document customer challenges, you'll be able to track the popularity of topics. Popular topics can then be repurposed in many, many ways. Once one topic has performed well—"How do I get my employees to use the new system?"—it can be sliced and diced in a bunch of different ways. You're not reinventing the wheel; you're just repurposing. There are probably about fifty different tweets you could do with that one blog post, or different types of downloads you could drive people to. It could become sponsored content in LinkedIn, and it could be a resource worth sharing. But what does a story about the company picnic do for your customer? Absolutely nothing.

TOOLS AND TACTICS FOR GREATNESS

If you're just getting into the game, the most important

tool that you need is an easy-to-use, easy-to-change, and easy-to-update content management system (CMS) for your website. In our case, we use WordPress. Once you create a good website, you need a good developer who is going to help you customize your content, your navigation, and your design based on your buyer persona. The CMS is the most important tool because that's going to allow you to test a whole bunch of things.

Make sure you have the Google Analytics code embedded on the site so you can track goals and conversions and understand what's happening with visitors. You then need some tools to drive traffic to the site. The spaces in which you tell your company story are important, but the amount of control you have over that varies. There's owned space, rented space, and paid space. (We'll cover this more in depth in chapter 5.)

A solid CMS that you can manipulate and use to test should be your top priority. Your website is your owned space. You can put some of your social media icons on there if they're active to help you engage with customers. You'll probably want to have a good stock photography account because you're going to want to create images that support your message. Access to good writers and designers who can help you craft the story of your business is also smart. Get all of that right before you start doing things like paying for sponsored ads on Twitter and Facebook, which would be your paid space.

A great way to come up with ideas for better content is to work backward from the questions you tend to get asked during the sales process and the topics or ideas you see in searches. This helps you outline your customers' objectives, key activities, the information they're consuming, the communication used, and the trajectory of their behavior. We designed a template for any company going through this process, which is described below.

Here's what I say to clients when we're going through the content workbook: Pretend they're not buying from you. Instead, they're buying from Company X, which sells, let's say, a project management tool. When they're trying to figure out what to get that will help their company, what are they looking at? What made them realize that they have a problem that needs solving? What are they trying to do? And ultimately, how can Company X earn their trust? Now, apply those same concepts to *your* company.

When a customer has a problem, what are they trying to do? The most important thing to them is not that they need this software—they may not know they need it yet—but that there's an issue they're dealing with that they want to solve.

When they realize the problem, what do they go look for? At this point, they still might not be looking for a project management software. Maybe they think that their project managers are terrible and they need to give them training; so maybe they've gone out to look for project management training. How do they search? I don't mean just online. Do they go talk to colleagues? What do they do?

Then they're going to create a list of choices and explore their options. That's when Company X can supply information about why training only solves part of the problem. They can show people, through good content, how selecting different choices will impact their business and why one of those choices might be a better project management tool. Now they are leading the conversation not based on features and functions of product, but from the perspective of the customer and how they see the problem.

We call this thought process creating a buyer map. It is the journey that your customers take to get from having a problem they're trying to solve to selecting you to solve it. This is how you achieve trust online with your prospective customers. Once you know the buyer journey, you can determine where the content should go or what the content should be about to help customers along the way and get them to an exploratory conversation.

In the case of one of my clients (they have a data mining tool), they compete against Oracle, IBM, and other big brand name companies. The biggest problem they had was a lack of name recognition. How could they gain their customers' trust if they weren't a brand name?

They needed to think about what their customers were trying to do and what goes wrong when they do it. From there, they can walk people through the process of how to solve their issue by providing content that outlines all of their options. When customers land on their home page, they'll see all the relevant content needed to make a decision.

A buyer map should be part of your tool kit and something you're always iterating on—because as you learn more about your customers and receive more sales insight, you'll realize they may need other things from you.

You need to paint the complete picture for your customer of what happens after they make a purchase—how the product will actually work, what real use case scenarios look like. The biggest problem in the software world is that they don't do this. They're so keen to show customers the product and get them on board that they lose sight of why buyers went to them for help in the first place.

That's where you can help out with content that shows videos of how easy it is to implement a solution—videos of how people are using it in their business today, how support works, and so on. And it doesn't matter if you're selling computer software or machinery or footwear for dogs. When you start talking about all the ways you can support your customer's journey on your website—even the journey they'll have after they buy something—you start to take away risk and concern that people have as they're researching a product or service. That's how you build trust in a digital world.

CONCLUSION

Everybody knows the story of the weekend handyman who likes to tinker but maybe doesn't quite have the right screwdriver to hang a picture or doesn't have the right tools to cut wood properly. But you know what? It's just good enough. He thinks, "I've got some hands-on knowledge. I can build a shelf. I'll just cut some wood and stick it up there." But then the next thing you know, the shelf is hanging there precariously—and then it all comes crashing down.

If you're okay with good enough and you're okay with the risk of a falling shelf because you didn't have the right tools and you didn't do the work properly, then that's fine.

You don't care. But if you truly want the shelf to survive, to support all your precious stuff without causing any damage or injury, then you need the proper tools and the proper process. You need to execute the task correctly in order to build long-term value into your digital strategy. And of course, you've got to put some things on the shelf to test it and make sure it works.

That's the difference between good enough and good. It's taking the time to create the right infrastructure with the right content and the right testing mechanisms to get you to the next stage.

→ Know why your customers buy from you.
→ Understand the journey your customers take to get to you—and to buy from you.
→ Create an infrastructure that allows you to test, iterate, blow up, and tinker until you get your content right.

CHAPTER 4

GETTING IT DONE VERSUS MAKING IT MATTER

• • • • •

Remember our caster client from chapter 1? For a long time, they thought the most important thing was the science behind how the caster was developed. We took them through the process of documenting their buyer map and determining the kinds of content that people are searching for around a product such as theirs. And what we realized was that people didn't care *how* the casters were developed—they cared about what a working caster meant to them. It's about that hospital bed that can easily glide across the floor and not injure hospital workers when the bed is pushed, or how much easier your job is when you don't have to fight to push a cart across the manufacturing shop floor.

Once we understood how to phrase value that was important to their customers, we helped them change the conversation. Their website communication used to be along the lines of, "Here's a product catalog. Here's what we sell. Which one do you want?" But now, the conversation is all about ergonomics and what happens to people when they have to push carts that don't move. Now their story is around why good design matters in real-world settings. We made the story about the people using the casters as opposed to just the casters themselves. Yet, when you go look at their competitors, all the competitors are just saying, "Here's our caster. Which one do you want it?" Our client is making their content matter by talking about a bigger story than their own casters.

A lot of people in manufacturing put their products online this way. At first the company thought they should be doing things that way as well. They had a new CEO who understood a lot of the customer journey. They had received some feedback from customers, so they were testing new ways to display their information. They kept putting new stuff on their home page and tested messaging and different concepts. They were putting things up, but they weren't measuring them to see how they were performing with their customers.

There is a company president whom I've worked with in

the past who uses this great analogy that I love. He says that when a parent goes out to buy her child a toy, she believes that toy will serve a purpose and provide her child with hours of play. So she gives the toy to the child, and what happens? The child has zero interest with it and just leaves the toy in the corner, never to be played with again. So how does this apply to the world of marketing? There is a clear distinction between customer experience (the parent) and user experience (the child).

Most companies don't realize the difference, so they start designing all these things around their "customer," not realizing that the user has very specific requirements and needs for what they do.

This is all fresh in my mind lately since we've been working with a company whose website is not designed for the customer (or the user). The website is designed for the senior management team and what they think is important to them. Every department is fighting to be on the home page, and there is no clear objective for the visitor to the site.

Part of the reason this company has struggled with building an effective website is that their products are not sold directly to the end user. They are sold through third-party resellers. So getting to know the customer has been tricky. They don't get direct access to their customers before the purchase. They only get to manage the customer after they buy. They understand the importance of a content plan, but getting to good content is a tricky process for this company.

Since they do serve the customer after purchase, senior management decided that building a customer portal for postpurchase would be a good thing. Seeing statement information online that mimics what they get in the mail was where they started their customer journey. So they built a minimum viable product—an MVP—just to get something up and see what would happen.

Their thinking was that everyone else has a customer portal, so they should, too! You may be familiar with this thinking: What's the smallest, cheapest, fastest product we can produce, from our perspective, to test this?

They invited close to a 100,000 customers to visit the portal and register. What they quickly learned was that the registration and log-in process was cumbersome. It was complicated, with a lot of opportunities for error. It wasn't one of those things where you just created a username and password and you were in. Instead you had to have the right names and account information. The call center was buzzing with questions about how to register.

Once people did log in, they realized that the only thing in the portal was something they were already receiving in the mail. And that was a frustrating realization to many customers. Was all that trouble to register worth it?

The original objective of the portal was for the company to stay on par with their competitors. They thought the route to do this was to build a portal. Once it existed, customers would automatically want to be there. What they weren't thinking through was that today's buyer has a journey that takes them all over the place. It's no longer a linear process where they log in through a gateway to get to information. Perhaps if they received something in the mail informing them of this new customer portal, then they would go directly to it. Ultimately, it's about delivering something to your customer that's better than what they're expecting.

You can't assume today where a customer starts their journey. You can't expect that a link received in the mail or email directing a person to a registration page is the only place they will go to access something. You have to consider all points of entry and why someone would do something. Forcing someone to follow your agenda rather than their own is a recipe for online disaster. And a bad web experience lowers a customer's opinion of you. It makes it seem as if the company didn't bother to ask their customers what they wanted or how something should work.

There are many different paths these days that can deliver a customer to you. You can't treat your site as if there's only one right way to get there. Because when you do, you're actually punishing those who have come to you from someplace else.

Getting it done quickly, hastily, without a process, so that you can get something going and move forward could actually be hurting you. Most likely, you'll have to repeat your work again and again until you get it right—and you'll lose people along the way. Creating a process to figure out what your customers actually want and delivering them a positive experience is what puts you further ahead than simply trying to get it done.

MERELY GETTING IT DONE

There are a lot of big companies with senior management teams dictating deadlines and visions, which then get passed down to management teams to execute. What ends up happening is, in the spirit of just trying to put up the next version of the website, nothing gets reworked in any major way that makes the experience better for the customer. The person making the changes may have a list they need to check off, and they may complete the changes, but is the website actually better without any improvements for the customer? I'd argue that it isn't.

In fact, it might even become worse in some ways. A lot of companies are stuck in this mind-set of "that's just the way we do it." Your boss tells you to do something and gives you a mandate, so you go do it. You don't think about it or push the envelope in any way with the kinds of questions that are important to the customer. Or maybe fixing what's wrong just seems too complex and difficult, so it's better to just get it done than to take the extra steps to actually make it better. Often, this seems like the easier path to take than to take a step back and think about it from the perspective of the customer.

This is "siloed thinking"—a mind-set that you can just do one thing and you can't deviate from that. For example, maybe this one person is responsible for promotional email marketing but doesn't think about it in terms of the landing pages on the website that have to exist for a customer to take a next step. Or maybe they're the developer and they created the functionality to make it work, but they're not thinking about what the content looks like that's supposed to get people there. This is how silos get created. You'll hear things like "I'm just the email marketing person" or "I'm just the SEO person." There's no leadership saying, "Well, you can't just be that, because that impacts a whole bunch of other things that are going on with the customer experience."

Siloed thinking means you're not thinking holistically. You're focused on one thing. You don't realize that there are other touch points and other things going on around you. When you have siloed thinking, you shortchange your customer.

I think there is a tendency in human nature to say, "Yeah, I know there might be a different way to do this, but that's not my job. My job is just to do X." We have a tendency to ignore the person whom we're doing something for, which means we don't build it for them. We find the fastest way to get it done. Maybe it's because a process doesn't exist to support the journey, or they don't think it exists. Over time choices are made because people are looking for the fastest way to get from point A to point B.

A lot of us live in fear of stepping outside the comfort zones of our defined roles. We fear questions like "Is this the best approach?" Perhaps we're afraid because we don't know if an alternative exists, or we're too nervous to ask tough questions. If we do, someone is going to force us to do more work.

So many companies I work with are stuck in get-it-done mode. They have this formulaic, paint-by-numbers approach to creating product sheets, with features and functions explained in great detail that don't add value to the buyer journey. They want to slice and dice information they've already posted on their website, thinking that maybe the reason it's not resonating comes down to an issue of semantics. But just slicing and dicing probably isn't going to get them much more value than what they've already got in the first generation of their website. If what they've been doing all along isn't working, doing more of it doesn't solve the problem—it amplifies it. Documenting what your customer cares about is the missing link. It's the secret sauce and the difference between getting it done and making it matter.

We often get clients who say, "My website is just not engaging. The content is not good. We don't think it performs very well. We need you to help us fix that problem."

But when we get into it, they are frustrated with how much work it takes. They say, "Well, we just want the website up in two weeks, and we'll just regurgitate some of the other product information we've used on other pages." They don't want to do the work.

So a company is trying to whip through the process faster

than they should because they don't realize how important some of these components are. They don't realize that it's important to take the time to figure out what content goes on each page, why it matters, and how to say it. They're frustrated with us, and they're pushing back, saying things like, "Well, what are you doing then? Why can't you figure this out for us?" We're in an awkward and uncomfortable place because they just don't get the value of going through the process. And unfortunately this is a pretty common issue we deal with when marketing teams try to outsource—they're just so used to getting it done.

Instead of sitting around as a group and internally fighting about what the content should be on a website, we should be asking our customers. We should be using a framework to get their feedback and make it matter versus just getting it done.

The biggest problem is that we keep doing the same thing over and over again and expecting different results. We're not going to get them. First of all, we're not going to get new results if we keep doing the same thing. Secondly, we're spending a lot of time and money. We think we're just getting it done, but we keep iterating on the wrong things. That's because we don't have a framework and a context from which to bring the customer into the dialogue.

What if we created a real buyer persona about who we were trying to engage? And what if we used that buyer persona as a framework to create content? We could create a blueprint for what works and build on it. Then we could go back and ask the customer, "Does this make sense?" We could test it and build on what works. Sure, it's a much longer process, and it might seem as if its more detailed and tougher to do, but it gets much better results. The biggest problem with a "let's just get it done" mentality is that we spend a whole bunch of time and money getting it done only to turn around and have to redo it again a year later because we didn't solve the problem, but we just got it done.

I see this happen a lot with people who are using email marketing as a batch-and-blast solution for their business. Sending out promotions twice a month isn't going to engage people, because there's only a small percentage of your audience that cares about the promotion. What about the rest of the people? The ones who keep deleting your emails every week? What are you doing for them?

Over the years I've realized that this fear to do something different, to change the way things have always been done, is really a fear of failure. People are so afraid to try something new online for fear that everyone will hate it. What if my boss doesn't like it? What if all my coworkers think it's bad? What does the customer think? What if I have to go back and try something else—won't that make my boss mad, since it's costing us more money?

If this sounds like you, it's time you changed your thinking. Your mind-set has to shift to be about having a continuous budget that allows you to constantly iterate and improve. That's the only way to make what you're doing matter to the customer. Getting it done is just putting a version up so that you have *something* and then walking away from it. Making it matter is publishing the first version, testing to see how it's doing, looking at the analytics, making adjustments, and constantly trying to make it better and more engaging for customers. Because what matters to your customers could change over time; and while that website you threw up could have been working at one point, it's unlikely that it still is. Stop going after the mole and thinking the mole is the problem. The problem is that you're trying to get it done when you need to be making it matter.

MAKING IT MATTER

Making it matter means creating an authentic, meaningful customer experience. It means that you've created a true connection with your customer. You've received feedback saying you're doing things right. When you truly make it matter, there are going to be moments when it feels hard, when it feels uncomfortable. There are going to be moments when you get frustrated and tempted to take the easy way out. But you have to resist this temptation, particularly as a content marketer, because taking the easy way out is a getting-it-done mentality. In order to create the structure that truly makes it matter, you have to come at it with a different approach.

The way to do this is to find ways to include your customers (and potential customers) in the marketing development process. You have to start somewhere, right? So start with a buyer persona:

- Who buys from you?
- What are their priorities?
- What are some obstacles that might keep them from buying?

In the past, we would have done one of two things: We would have gone to the product team asking for product information that we could slice and dice. Then we would have sat in meetings talking about how to present that information to our customers. And everyone would have their own opinion of how we should communicate with the customer. What I am advocating for here is for us to reverse engineer the process. Instead of starting with the product info, start with the person you want to reach and what they need to know. What is the level of difficulty required for customers to get the information they need from you? Once we know that, then we can backfill and create content that resonates with where customers are in their journey.

Some people do this well on their website. You can tell right away when you hit a site that has a clearly identified buying process that they want you to follow because they're trying to help you. Whereas other companies clearly don't have it figured out. They'll have multiple drop-down boxes, cram everything into the home page, and just hope you're going to click on something and figure it out for yourself. They're just putting stuff up there and hoping it'll work.

When you make it matter, you spend more time iterating against your best customer, testing what works and what doesn't, and iterating on the types of content that resonate the most. The data will show you how you're doing, because the time spent on the page will go up and the number of pages visited will go up. There are a lot of different metrics you can measure to see how you're doing. But if nobody comes to your website, it's because you just got it done and you threw something up there without making it matter.

One great company that's committed to great content as part of their marketing plan is Charity Water. They make their communication efforts personal by describing the kinds of people who don't have clean water in Third World countries and the impact that Charity Water has on them. When you go to their site, you know you're donating to a specific water well, a specific place, and ultimately to more stories like the ones you see from them. The way they do their content and storytelling shows that what they're doing as a company matters. They've changed the paradigm around information and the way we share content, and that to me is what really matters. I know that it takes a long time to get there, and you have to have a clearly defined value proposition and real clarity around what you're trying to do as a company to get there, but when you have that, you can make a difference with your content.

CONCLUSION

The story about the caster manufacturers in the beginning of this chapter makes me so happy because they are trying to make content that matters. They realized that the great thing about these casters has nothing to do with the casters—instead it's about the experience of being able to move things with ease. Think about how annoying it is when you have a shopping cart with a wheel that doesn't work. You're paying attention to that wheel. But when the wheels are running smoothly, you're not thinking about them at all. Now when this caster company communicates through content, the most successful stories they share are the ones where people aren't thinking about the wheels, but rather what moving wheels can help them do. This is what resonates with their customers.

I've worked with lots of marketers who get this right, who've embraced it and have been grateful for this process of test, rework, focus, and iterate. Then I've worked with others who have railed against it because they want to get their product info on a website and they think that's all that matters. They resist because this is a different way of thinking.

There's a quotation I love by Jay Behr: "Don't make content; make a difference." He's a great, thoughtful guy in the world of content marketing. "We don't need more content marketers," he says. "We need people who have a passion to make connections." The difference between getting it done and making it matter is that when you make it matter, you make a connection. When you get it done, you're just posting things online. His point is that the mission of content is to be an emotional bridge between business and consumers. When you just get it done, you don't create that emotional bridge. So instead of just making content—which is what a vast majority of people do when they build their website—you need to make content that matters.

> → Am I putting myself in the customers' shoes and making this matter, or am I just getting it done?
> → Am I proud of this work, or did I just rush through it to get something—anything—up online?
> → Test to see if what you're doing is working—and if it's not, pivot and try again.

DON'T WASTE TIME ON SOCIAL MEDIA

• • • • •

I want you to read this title in two different ways...

Don't *waste* time on social media.

Don't waste *time* on social media.

The first is a comment about how you spend time in social media for your business. I am suggesting with this chapter heading that even though people spend a lot of time in social media, they are not productive, because they are either in the wrong place or doing the wrong thing.

The second way of reading the heading suggests that, depending on what you sell and who you sell to, without spending time to get your content right, you are wasting time in social media.

A lot of companies today think that in order to be relevant to their customers, they need to be on social media. If you've set up a social media account just because you think you "have to," then you have the wrong idea. Without a plan and an understanding for how social media can be used as a tool, for a lot of businesses it just winds up being filler—an empty attempt to appear current that actually has the inverse effect.

I would love to have access to the data for all the companies that insist on putting social media icons in the top right-hand corner of their website. Why do people still do this? This is something I continue to see with many of my clients. A financial institution we worked with recently is a prime example. I challenged them to think about why they insisted the icon should be on their site. When I clicked on their Facebook icon, I discovered that the content they posted was neither helpful nor thoughtful. They'd shared a story about "27 uses for the iPhone," which had nothing to do with banking whatsoever. How is that content helpful to their customers? It isn't. If you're sharing content via social media that isn't useful or applicable to your customers, then what's the point?

> **Confession time**—I really dislike social media. I understand its social impact over the last five years. I understand why people like it (individuals), and I get its allure, but it has made us lazy thinkers and it is rife with inaccurate information. I also don't think that business owners truly understand the role it plays in their business.

The companies who are guilty of this behavior think that by putting an icon up on their home page or by posting stories onto their Facebook wall, they're able to have some skin in the game. They think being relevant is all about being in the right places. What they fail to understand is that being in the right places is only half of it. You have to supply your audience with content that is relevant to them and that builds a bridge back to you.

I've spoken to three different nonprofit groups recently, and they all say the same thing: "If I could just get a campaign to go viral on social media, that would really help us with donations." But when you talk to people who have had a successful viral media campaign, with a few exceptions, these don't produce the record numbers of donations everyone is hoping for. The odds are just incredibly against you. But why aren't these social campaigns producing the kinds of results the nonprofits want? You have to look at the medium. People are on Twitter because they're looking for news, looking to keep up with the folks they follow, or to take a sort of cultural pulse for what people are talking about. Even if they see something that's cool and they share it, it's unlikely that they're going to take the time to click through to the company website connected to that product. There is an element of cultural currency to sharing something on social media that can happen without shelling out any real dollars.

The reason people are so hesitant and resistant to click through to a company website from social media is because the process is often broken. In the case of the nonprofits I spoke with, most of them don't optimize their website for mobile. Without a true mobile application to your donation process, you are left sending someone to a website that often takes fifty clicks in to figure out how to navigate and what to do. Then you're lost. For sites like this, there should be exactly one click required—a *donate* button—in order to optimize the experience for the desired outcome with a dead-simple process to follow and various ways to pay.

When the nonprofit I discussed in chapter 3 did their social campaign and didn't raise any money, they came to us scratching their heads. The mistake they made was that they didn't consider the medium they were using and what its main purpose has become. You have to think about how people are interacting on social media and then capitalize on what's already happening rather than jumping on social media and trying to make it do something different. If it's not conducive to fundraising, then it's not going to be a successful fundraising tool.

The point of social media is to be social—it's to engage people without any expectation for something in return (it's just the "SEE" stage of the journey). The problem with this for businesses is that they see social media as a channel for programming and they expect something in return. They expect leads. They expect sales. They think if they're on Twitter, or Facebook, or Instagram, or Snapchat, then they'll get a lot of followers, and that will translate to new or continued business. But that's not why these platforms exist, and that's certainly not why people are going to them.

Social media is a great place for a company to listen—to hear the conversations happening around their products, their competitors, or simply within an audience of the people they see as potential customers. It's a way to find out what matters to people, to do research about content that connects. And it's excellent for reading the latest headlines. Depending on the channel, and how the channel gets used, it can be quite powerful. Social media has a great purpose when it's used in its truest form, but unfortunately most companies aren't looking at it that way.

Most companies see social media as a place to mass-market. They see it as a replacement to *The New York Times*. They see it as a platform of people just waiting for them. They think that they need to be there as a way to attract an audience to their business, but they're not thinking about *how* to engage them and *how* to use it as a content tool.

Without getting the foundation right, without understanding how the audience *wants* companies to interact with them, most are just spinning their wheels. But the biggest mistake business owners make is to create a social media account and then fail to think about the customer's journey and what happens once they click through to the company website. I am willing to bet there's been a lot of money lost because someone didn't think through what happens once a customer goes from a Facebook page to a company website and what that journey should look like in order to lead to a sale.

I've noticed a trend among some blogs lately of removing the ability for commenting, since places like Twitter or Facebook are better venues for that kind of dialogue. In comment sections, the conversation tends to go a bit off the rails, so moving the conversation elsewhere means it won't detract from the story or the post. Do those blogs still possess the ability to have comments? Sure—it's not that they're removing the functionality; it's simply that they're restricting it. But just because you can do something doesn't mean you should. And the same thing applies to creating social media accounts for your business.

There is a false sense of security in thinking that if you create all these social media accounts—LinkedIn, Facebook, Google Plus, Twitter, Instagram, Snapchat, and so on—then you will be able to be everywhere at once. But the reality is that you can't be everywhere, and you shouldn't be everywhere. And trying to be everywhere at once means you're never fully present in any one place.

It's like telling your daughter that you will go to her dance recital, but all you do is sit in the parking lot because you're busy taking a call. You may be there in the physical sense, but you're not present. Sitting in the parking lot isn't the same thing as watching her perform. The same thing goes for joining all these social media networks and posting their icons on your home page. How good can you really be at being in all those places at once? If your business doesn't lend itself to pictures, then maybe Pinterest and Instagram aren't for you. If you can't produce decent-quality videos regularly, then YouTube probably isn't your thing. This is the way you should be thinking about social media rather than trying to join every available network in the hopes that simply being there will be enough.

The downfall to trying to be on all these channels—and not doing any one of them particularly well—is that when people do find you there, they're going to be let down. You haven't done anything to help yourself stand out. People think that because there are all these online tools, each social media account is a faceless and nameless entity—just a digital extension of the brand. But what they forget is that there is a personal aspect to this. Social media should be a place to learn, get educated, and share. I've personally stayed off much of social media because I just don't feel I can have a meaningful conversation there. And yet, I feel tremendous pressure to be on all these channels for business reasons. I get it—that need to be everywhere is powerful!

Another misstep I've seen with companies trying to leverage social media is when they have a LinkedIn page or a Facebook account but fail to follow any of their customers or any of the companies they have relationships with. They think that just because they're there, it counts. But if they're not even following their own customers, then how can they have an authentic and meaningful conversation in that space?

It's simply unrealistic to think that a large amount of followers is going to equate to more sales. There seems to be an unrealistic expectation today about that. Many businesses think it should work that way, but it's just not the case. We have a client who runs a start-up selling a fantastic product. It's drum lessons for drummers, and he has amassed a ton of followers through his Instagram account because he focuses on a niche and something that ties a community together—drum kits. There are a lot of drum enthusiasts out there who love looking at drum kits. His content connects with people, and he has a great story to tell. It's wonderful.

Recently, he came to me because he was frustrated. "Why doesn't 40,000 followers on Instagram equate to sales?" he wanted to know. He thought that if he had all these followers, if he was posting regularly, and if people were engaged with what he was doing on social media, then that should translate into sales.

I asked him to think about a brand for a minute that he loves. Of course he mentioned a brand of drum kits that was very exclusive and high-end. I asked if he followed them on social media. He said only on one social media outlet because he liked the pictures and he liked to "look." "So you are 'just browsing,'" I suggested, and then asked if he would ever buy from this company. He agreed he would if he won the lottery. Next I asked him what the next step would be if he did win the lottery and was able to purchase a kit. He thought about this for a moment and realized that he would go right to the company website and look up retailers that he could visit in his vicinity. So what role does Instagram play in the sale of the drum kit? He realized that it helps out when people are "just looking," but that the real journey would start on the company website and the "find retailers" tab.

So here is where I want you to start as a business person trying to use social media. Start with the buyer journey. Map out how someone buys a product or service like yours, and decide what role social media plays in that journey.

You have to look at the spectrum of tools available to you and be realistic about the purpose of each. In its simplest sense, social media is for companies to be noticed. It is a great way to communicate directly with your customer base, to listen to what they're saying, and to get feedback in real time. For customers, it's a way to find out more about you, to get a sense of what you're all about, and to see what others are saying to, about, or with you. How that goes then determines if they'll take the next step with you. If they want to learn more and if they're interested, then they'll take action by going to your website or reaching out to salespeople or reading your blog posts.

There is an unrealistic expectation about what social media can actually do for your business. We all need to wrap our heads around that—above everything else. In addition to this, the quality of our conversations goes down when we're trying to have too many conversations at the same time. Try it: Engage five different people in conversation at the same time, on five different topics, and see how well it goes. Compared with only one conversation, I'm guessing the quality of engagement on your part would drop drastically—and put off those you're attempting to speak to. This is exactly what happens when you try to be everywhere on social media.

The power of social media is huge. There is no cheaper, faster platform for engaging with people, talking to them, listening to them, sharing content, and getting immediate feedback. This has been an integral part to my speaking engagements. I'll talk at a conference and then go on Twitter after and get great feedback via those who were in the audience. Feedback is a gift, and I wouldn't have heard as much of it if Twitter didn't exist. The real-time nature of Twitter and other social media can be incredible for sharing information. But you have to be a constant participant in order to reap the benefits.

We worked with a software company not too long ago and

helped them develop a new version of their website with better content that we hoped would better support the buyer journey and get better results. We went through our upfront methodology with them, and it became apparent that they were pretty halfhearted about it. They didn't want to do the work to understand the buyer journey, nor were they too keen to move away from traditional features and function selling. In other words, they weren't that keen to give their company a voice.

There's a newness and a timeliness to social media. A lot of people use Twitter as their news feed: What's new? What's happening now? If all you're doing is pushing out product information over, and over, and over, and over again, that's stale. That's old. Why would somebody want to keep looking at that? There has to be something fresh in the discussion, but there can't be if all you keep doing is talking about the same five features and functions of your product over and over again. Think about what matters to your customers, do a test, and then do more of what works.

This software company was stuck in an old way of thinking—they thought that things that were most important to them were also going to be the things that would resonate with their consumers. And as we know, this is just not the case. They were stuck in a way of thinking that hadn't evolved. They weren't thinking about the customer journey and what the customer would need to know from them in order to move forward with making a purchase.

So we explained this to them, about how posting relevant regular content as a way to have a conversation with customers is the way to win. But they still didn't want to do the work. They didn't want to do the research and figure out the topics that matter to their customers. Instead they just wanted to say, "Here's what I'm selling, are you ready to buy?" So they told us they weren't going to work with us anymore, that they heard what we were saying but they were going to go in a different direction. And you know what that direction was? They hired someone to be in charge of their social media. They told us they thought being more active on social media was a better way for them to *sell*.

A few years back you saw a lot of people selling social media services. These "social media professionals" promised they could take over a company's social media accounts and help them with their bottom line. They assured companies that they would drive leads to their website, simply by increasing their presence on social media. So this software company hired a guy to run their social media accounts, and he was supposed to build up their presence online, drive leads to their website, and increase sales. And guess what? After he was there about a

month and got everything set up, he finally raised his hand
to ask a question and it went a little something like this:

"What content should I share?"

"Talk about the product!"

"I don't think that's going to fly."

"Why not?"

*"People aren't interested in talking about that—do you
have anything else I can talk about?"*

So he tried to figure out what he should be talking about:
Were there things for people to download and try out, was
there content from speeches the higher-ups had done, or
were there any blog posts that he could point to? He was
basically following our road map, the one that we tried
to take them through in the first place.

"You're just supposed to get us followers," they told him.
They didn't understand the nuances of what it means to
be truly social, about having a conversation with people
rather than just talking at them. I'll give it to the guy—he
tried. He took a stab at it for six months before they fired
him because they weren't getting the results they wanted.

They figured their message must be what was broken, so after they let him go, they went to a PR agency and asked them to create some thirty-second clips they could use on their website and in social media.

The PR company they hired—who is very good, by the way—came up with some interesting messages for them, but had no idea how to apply them to the website because there was still no framework for what their customer wanted. So they fired them, too! Then they came back to us.

"Okay, we still have a nonperforming website," they said. "We're not driving leads, and we've tried all these other things. What do we do now?"

So we told them that they need to return to our process and actually do it this time. They needed to understand their value proposition—why someone would pick them over all the other options that are available. It's important what their customer thinks, not what the company thinks. Once they got an understanding of that, then we could help them create a story that's bigger than just the product, one that encompasses what they are all about and how their vision could help make their customers' lives better.

After doing all this, we rolled up our sleeves and figured

out a series of blog topics and a downloadable piece of content that they could use in their social media communication. We helped them figure out a way to have a conversation with their customers so they could see who cared about it. The truth is, some people might not care about what you're saying. That's okay! But for the people who do care and who are responding to your message, it gives you valuable feedback on what's working and what to do more of. That's all a part of testing, trying, and reiterating.

We did all this with them, and soon it started to work. They were getting the right kind of traffic back to their site, and the right kind of people were inquiring about their solution.

But they still weren't happy—they wanted more. If they wanted to keep having this kind of success with their content, then they would need to expand the conversation and take the time to write more original content. They started small and were ready to build. So they kept telling a better story, using winning topics in new ways, and finding different ways to reiterate on the conversations that were proving positive. They were posting regularly, too, which is important.

We encouraged the head of sales to do videos taking

people through a high level demo of the product, a natural next step. From there they were able to grow their efforts more and more. And when things worked—like posting a price list on their site—we helped them come up with new ways to package the product so it would stay relevant. (In fact, that continues to be the most popular page on their website.) Once they had their content down to a science (and it is a science!), that's when things like public relations and social media started to work. Having that foundation is tantamount to communicating well with customers.

Thinking that getting followers on social media will fix all of your problems is just so wrong. There are other steps you need to take first in order to make social media work for you. And when you do take those steps, you'll find that everything else gets better.

Social media is about building relationships, and just like building relationships in the real world, this takes time and energy and habitual contact. It's neither fast nor easy. The idea of just dabbling, just dipping your toe in to see how it feels, is not a good one. Not only do you need to be where you customers are, but you need to take the time and make an effort to connect.

Back in the 1990s, I worked as a press secretary to a federal cabinet minister in Canada, and every year at Christmas our Prime Minister Brian Mulroney would take the time to personally call everyone in his Rolodex. I know this for a fact because I was the one who coordinated receiving the calls two years in a row. So he'd go through his contact database and make these calls and would wish people a Merry Christmas. Some he would spend more time chatting with, but it was usually just some light pleasantries asking about how things were going with them. Think about how long that must have taken! But he did it—he rolled up his sleeves, and he did it.

He knew that it was important and that it was his way to touch base with people he hadn't spoken to in a while. It was more than just sending a Christmas card. He called his cabinet ministers. He called all the people in parliament. He called all the people who had worked on his fundraising campaign. He went through the entire Rolodex. It was quite impressive.

Fast-forward to today and how we maintain connections with people—we can use social networking sites such as Facebook and LinkedIn in the same way. Try to reach out personally to people by sharing information with them—such as by sharing a link they might like or a video. It takes time, and it means you need to know people, and it means you need to get intimate. You can't just leave it at a surface level for it to be authentic. That's neither easy, nor fast, nor cheap. But it delivers results.

BE WHERE YOUR CUSTOMERS ARE

Understanding where your customers are and why they're there is integral to creating a connection with them. In order to do this, you must understand three distinct marketing channels. I'll cover this more in depth in chapter 6 (Get Your Own Space Right First), but here's the quick and dirty intro to how it works.

OWNED: This is a channel that you have complete control over. It's your website, your newsletter, your blog—all things where you can control the story in its entirely. You can manage the vision, and you can select which stories you want to tell. You own this space. It's a space people expect you to have. In today's day and age, everyone has to have an owned space (their website) in order to be considered relevant. When people are looking for you (or for companies like you), they're going to see what you have on your website and if it's intriguing or appealing. If it is, they might sign up for something. You control the entire process.

RENTED: This channel has some level of ownership, but not entirely. This is where social media falls. You may be able to create the Twitter account, and have control over what you post, but you have no way to control what others say about you here. There are some pretty big limitations to what you can do here.

PAID: In this channel, you can be very specific about where you want to be by using things like AdWords or sponsored links on Google, other sponsored content, or even ad targeting. There are a lot of new ways to pay for placement online, but people know and can see that you've paid for that placement. And so it can feel inauthentic. In the same way people don't like commercials on TV—they wish they could just get back to their show—they've accepted that they're there and that companies are paying to be there. There are some moments when paid channels are a good thing, especially when it blurs the lines between editorial and advertorial and is done in a way that looks more like a conversation rather than just pure advertising.

All of these channels are important in their own right, but it's the combination of the three that helps you win online. How much of a percentage you allot to each is dependent on who your customers are and where they are. For example, say you sell a very specific product that has a very specific keyword attached to it. If you know that your customers use a search engine to find that product, and that they're going to want to find a website giving

The Content Roadmap

Emotional connection for the buyer (based on buyer persona): ???______________

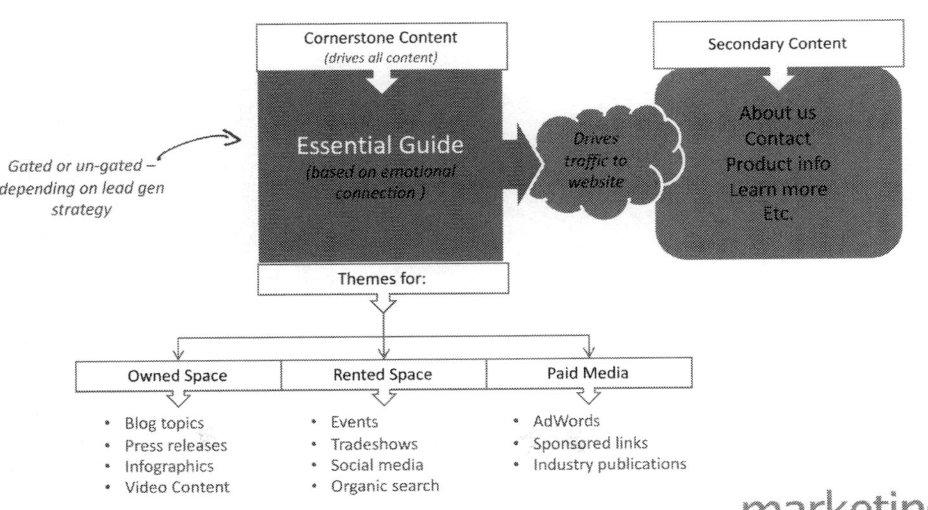

more information, then paying to rank higher in searches might be right for you.

It's so important to wrap your head around these three things because you can't just be a one-trick pony anymore. Just being on social media (rented) isn't going to be enough—the same way that just being on paid search (paid) or just having a website (owned) isn't going to be enough either. I've worked with companies who still think that all of their leads are going to come from cold-calling. The times have changed, people! And in order to stay relevant and alive, you've got to change with them.

CONCLUSION

Ask yourself: Do you really want to spend time in this rented space of social media when it's not going to help you with your main objective?

Social media takes way more time and thought than most people realize. If you're using social media to connect with friends and family in lieu of picking up the phone and talking to them, then social media is important. But as a business tool, it's going to take way more thought, time, and resources than you realize.

At the end of the day, it's just one piece of the overall

puzzle, and it's just one channel. Even if you get your rented space right, you're still going to need to get your owned and paid spaces right, too. It's a piece, but it's not the whole pie. So you need to ask yourself how much time you're willing to spend there. If you're willing to spend a considerable chunk of time, then there's nothing wrong with that, but you need to spend time in the right places doing the right things.

If you have a big community that you want to connect with, and you want to be part of that conversation and hear what's going on, and you've got lots of exciting things to share, then social media works really well. For some specific niches, like the gaming community or the tech industry, for example, social media is an incredible way to tap into a bigger community of shared interests and ideas.

But for small businesses, it's a much harder nut to crack. So don't waste *time*—and don't *waste* time. It's important to take stock of *why* you're there. Why does it matter to your customers? What are you doing to engage? How are you socializing? It's the first stage in the SEE/DO/THINK/ CARE approach. Social media is part of that first stage. If people see what you're doing and like it, then they may take action. But at the end of the day, it's not contributing much to your overall conversion strategy, so you need to think about how important it is for you to be there.

➡ What matters to your customers?

➡ What are you doing on social media to engage them?

➡ Why are you there?

CHAPTER 6

GET YOUR OWN SPACE RIGHT FIRST

In the previous chapter, I spoke about some of the challenges of playing in the rented space of social media. Meanwhile, companies often neglect their owned space: their company website.

The Internet allows us all these different ways to hide. You can hide behind your email, your website, and anonymous commenting sections, because you never have to look someone in the eye while posting, searching, and interacting. These shrouded interactions mean that you also don't know how someone is reacting to your website or to your content. Google has actually shifted their algorithms as of late to function in favor of the human. When content performs well on a personal level, when it has on-page engagement—that sends a message to Google that it is good content. But sadly, not many businesses are rising to meet the challenge. So who's to blame? Man or machine?

I'd like to share a little story with you about trying—and that's the keyword here—to order Chinese food. It all started with a little Google search for Chinese food delivery in Unionville, which is the neighborhood I had just moved to within my city of Toronto. The first three sites had PDFs of menus. Many were not in English, and not one included delivery times or payment terms in a helpful way. These small businesses were communicating a message to me, as a consumer, that they didn't want my business. That's the impression that I got, at least.

Then I came across a website that was laid out very well. It was easy to navigate, with friendly content, and a nice mobile interface. The prices, menu options, and delivery times were all clearly posted, and everything was clear and straightforward. So I called them and placed my order.

As it turns out, I had placed an order for delivery at a restaurant in Unionville, Connecticut. They called me back about fifteen minutes later, laughing, and informed me that I was a little bit outside their delivery distance (to put it mildly). So how was it that their restaurant was the fourth search result that came up for me on Google? The reason they were getting such a high ranking for their site was because of its usability. It was crazy to me that the site for their restaurant, which was some eight hours and 798 kilometers away from me, was beating out sites for other restaurants that were just up the block from my house.

GET YOUR OWN SPACE RIGHT

At the end of the day, people hate change. It's just so much easier to print a brochure (or post a PDF menu) than it is to take the time to consider a customer's journey. But the most essential thing to do—and the biggest takeaway from reading this book—is to consider your customer's journey. Ask yourself questions like this when building your website: Who is going to come here? What kind of content do they need or want to consume? What is the most obvious information they're going to need to understand first? As business owners, we want all of this stuff to be happening with sales leads and social media and outreach, but we're not considering that at the end of the day the most important thing is that we're being clear, engaging, and informative in the space we own. And if we're not those things in the customer's eyes, then we're nowhere.

When I go to a website with bad content navigation, I feel as if it's screaming at me, "We don't want your business!" That's the message that I'm receiving as a user of that website. And as a customer, it's hard to trust a business who doesn't get their owned space right. But for all the companies we work with who are willing to get their hands dirty and do the work to make their website better for their customers, there are still those clients who don't want to.

We had a client like that once, and it was a very challenging experience and put us in a very awkward place. We had given them the outline for the content map, their keywords, what kinds of content they should building—the usual deal. So we started to write stuff for them so they could get a sense for the tone, and there were all these places where they needed to fill in the details of how or why something worked the way it did. And when we asked them to do that, they got mad. They didn't want to do the work! "You should be writing this," they said. "What are we paying you for?" That was their attitude toward the whole thing, because they didn't want to roll up their sleeves. And this leads to a crucial message that we always tell our customers now before they hire us: Understanding your customer can't be outsourced. *You* need to own that. And you need a process that's part of a framework that helps you develop good content. Good content can't be made up—it needs to be based on the specific research you've done to understand your customer's journey.

A good example of a company getting their space right is the personalized paper and invitation site Minted. They've presented themselves in such a way that makes it so easy to use their service. It's a simple, easy-to-use format that allows you to insert your own personal photos and in essence design your own product online. They've thought through their customer's process, and their website walks you through step-by-step and without any clunkiness to the application. The whole experience of doing business with them is very smooth and streamlined. Inbound marketing platform HubSpot is another company that has a great web presence. Granted, I know that's what they sell for a living, but they've just done such a great job with their website, making complex technology easy to understand.

There are a few key things we can learn from companies that create a good customer service experience via their website. First and foremost, they've made choices. They haven't tried to be all things to all people, and they orient you pretty quickly as to whether or not this site is for you, or whether or not their product is for you. They do a good job of creating that singular moment that either propels you to continue or turns you away.

The second thing they do is they tell a story bigger than themselves. The reason I like Charity Water's website so much is because they quickly orient you to the reason why the subject matter is so important, and the understanding of why they do what they do is immediate once you visit. I love the fact that they get you quickly to a story that you're interested in hearing. Finally, a good website leads you to a natural conclusion of what you should do next. You shouldn't be expected to just randomly click around on stuff or try to sort through what all the drop-down boxes are. Every page needs an action and a reaction that leads you to a logical next step—things like donate, watch a video, and so on.

You want to continue to tell your story until someone reaches the point where it resonates and they're inspired to take action or make a purchase. Whatever the journey, it's the storytelling—whether it's showing other people using the product, giving examples, or simply leading them in the right direction—that propels them to take a specific action. So, you want to have guided them to get there.

I went to a site recently for a company in the UK whose primary product is a marketing automation tool. I don't hear from this company very often, so when I got an email from them I actually paid attention. But when I clicked through from their email, instead of getting some kind of download or something that was going to guide me, I was met with a huge landing page filled with long copy, where every two paragraphs there was a button that said "Try now" or "Try for 60 days." They were constantly trying to sell me something. This is not a great tactic if you want customers to learn from you, because this kind of constant badgering stands in the way of gaining a consumer's trust.

There's a time and a place for each one of those strategies, but if you try to get somebody to take some kind of action too soon, and that action seems to be about you and not them, you'll lose them. (I'll cover this topic more in depth in chapter 7: Don't Propose on the First Date.) What you should be doing is taking your customer on a subtle journey to help them develop trust, then ask about what they might want to do next in a way that works for them, and not just make them feel like you're trying to sell them something. That's why getting the content right on your website is so important. People need to get to know you, and you need to give them that opportunity before you ask them to do something.

Like it or not, people in this day and age expect you to have a website. Even if you're the tiny, mom-and-pop Chinese food restaurant down the street that I spoke about in chapter 6, people expect you to have a presence online. And those who don't are hurting themselves from a business perspective.

When a customer visits your website, they expect it to be cleanly designed, well put together, organized, and easy to navigate immediately from the moment he or she visits it. This is the most important thing you can do and the most important place for you to start. It's a place you own, so you can control how you set it up. You have the opportunity to do the work so you can own it. It's imperative that you meet your customers' website expectations—when you do, it's a good reflection on your company and helps keep customers interested in you.

When WordPress was first taking off, all the pundits said that if you had a blog, you'd never need a website. But that wasn't necessarily true then, and it's certainly not true now. People need different types of content consumed in different ways and at different times. Later, businesses were told that they needed to be on Facebook, and that doing so would negate the need for a company website. "You can just put it all on Facebook," some said. But that's not an owned space—you can't control how the page looks or how it's set up or how you're going to guide someone through your content. It's a rented space that you can never truly own. And in the case of social media sites like Facebook, the rules are constantly changing to suit their purposes, not yours.

The biggest problem most people have is that they don't

know where to start. There are some fantastic services available today that make building your own website easy and relatively pain-free. But you can't force-feed a customer journey through someone else's idea of what a website should look like. The most important thing you can do is to take the time to understand your customer's journey and then present your information in a way that caters to that process. Take the time to think about how you want to present your information, and you'll have a powerful web presence that will engage your audience and convert them to customers.

BUYER JOURNEY

It's human nature to want to talk about ourselves, what we do, and the product or service we offer. That's an easy place to start for most people, but it's the wrong place to start. Instead, ask yourself why you started your business. Work on articulating your vision for who you are and what you're trying to do. Think about the kinds of customers you want and how your product or service helps to make their lives better. What makes you different from the rest of the competition? Answering all these questions through the content on your website, and therefore educating your customers on what you're all about, is far more engaging and interesting than simply listing details about your product or service. Doing this kind of deep dive means that you're no longer just guessing. Get into the *why*, and it will lead your customers to *buy*.[9]

BUYER RESEARCH

Too many people confuse the buyer journey with their sales process. That is not the buying process. The buying process starts from their perspective and how they see the problem they are trying to solve. They have an issue, either in their own business or in their personal life, and they're trying to find ways to fix it. So they do research—either online or by asking around—and they try to find out what their options are. Most of the time, this phase is just a simple Google search. Anywhere from 55 to 75 percent of the buyer journey has happened before you, the business owner, even know that person is looking. By the time he gets to you, he's already weighing his options and figuring out what his choices are.

9   According to Simon Sinek, the fundamental difference between the "Apples" of the world and everyone else is that they start with "why." *What does that even mean?* To explain this concept, Sinek has developed what he calls the "Golden Circle." The golden circle has three layers:

Why—This is the core belief of the business. It's *why* the business exists.
How—This is *how* the business fulfills that core belief.
What—This is *what* the company does to fulfill that core belief.

Although it sounds simple, what Sinek found is that most companies do their marketing backward. They start with their "what" and then move to "how" they do it. Most of these companies neglect to even mention *why* they do what they do. More alarmingly, many of them don't even know why they do what they do!

For more, visit: https://www.ted.com/talks/
simon_sinek_how_great_leaders_inspire_action?language=en

BUYER EVALUATION

Then, the buyer evaluates. He makes a short list (even just in his head) about who his top picks are. So he starts to think about the questions he wants to ask and the specifics he needs to learn in order to make his decision.

Then he purchases, receives the product or service, and experiences what it does. Then one of two things happens: he either becomes a customer for life because the experience he's had was so good and the process was one that generated trust and comfort, or he didn't have a positive experience and starts the process all over again with someone else.

We follow the buyer journey according to how it's mapped to determine what to do at different stages from a sales perspective, but a lot of times we jump too soon to a sales tactic when somebody might only be in search mode. Say the customer is in search mode and the first thing on your website is "Free Trial." It's off-putting to keep pushing her to a conversion if she's still in the research phase of her journey. I've worked with a lot of technology companies where this was the case.

You have to think about what is going on with your customers. If all you're doing is offering them that free trial, and they're still in research mode, then wouldn't it be better to offer them a comparison chart showing how you stack up against the competition? You don't even need to name your competitors. Simply show them the different ways others have solved this problem and what solutions are available for them. Then have your name in a list of choices to help them understand their options.

BUYER CONFIRMATION

Another very important part of the customer journey is determining when you ask for their information—things like a name, phone number, or email address—and when you don't. I was doing research recently while shopping for a new blender, and on one company website I found a free download showing the comparisons between one brand and its competitors. And it was completely non-gated, which means they didn't ask me for any personal information in order for me to access and download this one-page document. That was a good call on their part, because had they asked for my personal information too soon, I wouldn't have trusted them, and I would have immediately had my guard up. While I was in search mode, I didn't want to think about what this person was trying to sell me, and if they had tried to do so, it would have turned me off.

There are ways to have gated content without making it seem like a ploy just to get you to buy. In this same example of blender shopping, they could have engaged me with a recipe book for the blender and gated it that so I had to enter my name and email in order to get it. There is value in that information, so that makes sense. As it turned out, when I did end up looking for recipes, one of the blender companies had a weekly recipe email newsletter, which I was more than happy to supply my email address for and receive. After all, this was exactly what I was looking for! Now, they make a connection with me constantly by delivering information I want to my inbox on a regular basis. Even though I might not be in the market to buy more from them now—after all, I just bought their blender—they're creating a connection between me and their brand that tethers me to them in the long term. It will be another ten years before I need to buy another blender, so there's no immediate return for them to keep sending me recipes, but they're invested in the relationship, and that will certainly pay off in referrals to friends and extended brand loyalty.

We have a client who manufactures Lucite products—that heavy-duty acrylic that makes it easy to suspend anything inside a clear block. They get asked all the time if they can do things like trophies or memorabilia embedment so that a moment can be preserved forever. An oil and gas company asked them to suspend drops of crude oil in their Lucite after they had struck oil at a location. Also, a police officer wanted his badge embedded after thirty years on the force. There are all these amazing things you can do with their technology, so they created a catalog showing all these examples of their custom work and how the pricing is set up. When they first put the catalog on the website, they did not gate it. But we started to see all this amazing activity on that part of their website, so it became obvious that this was important information to people. We saw how many pages people had gone to before they hit the pricing information and what they had to go through on the site to even get to this catalog in the first place. It was quite the journey to get to this great piece of content. Since the data and analytics (see chapter 2) were telling us this content had great value, we decided to gate it. And you know what? Their lead generation went through the roof.

They were getting calls before they gated their catalog, but now they were getting increased engagement through email. This meant we could continue to gain value by building in content via blog posts. It wasn't that they were pushing people to buy; rather, they were just pushing out content every couple of weeks that featured another cool idea of something you can do with Lucite. It was a way to keep pulling customers into something that they'd already expressed interest in. Gating content at the right place and the right time on a website can be very important to the whole buyer journey.

We work with a lot of clients who have a very complex product or service to sell. When I say complex, I mean there is a lot to understand and there are a lot of moving parts. This means that the cycle to get from research to sale is pretty long—it's not as easy as buying a blender.

The sales process is quite different. What is really difficult with some of these clients is helping them realize that the problem that they're solving is a really difficult problem, and they've provided a really smart solution. They're usually smart people who have really thought it through, but they have a very intellectual response to why their product or service matters. But you can't get buy-in until you've created an emotional connection. If you don't create that emotional connection, you haven't earned the right to provide an intellectual answer. People don't want to take the time to understand it if you haven't made that connection first.

You have to establish quickly that you and your customers share a similar view on the world, that you both have identified this problem that needs fixing, and you're just the one to fix it. A lot of people jump to the nuts and bolts of how something works or the big-picture explanation of how their solution fits into the world. But it's too soon for that. First, you have to foster an emotional connection as a trigger that allows people to relate. Until you do that, they won't read on. They won't click through. They won't do anything with the content, because you haven't earned the right yet. But once you've established that connection, then you'll be allowed to have a more intellectual conversation with your customers about how you're going to fix the problem.

There's an accounting company in Canada, called Fresh-Books, whose target audience is small business owners and entrepreneurs like myself looking for solutions to do invoicing better. It's a great success story because they've done really well, and a big part of that has to do with how they create an emotional connection with their customers. When they first launched, their home page was pretty simple: a shoebox overflowing with receipts. And when I saw that image, it instantly clicked with me. It was exactly how my bookkeeping looked at the time. In fact, back then we were using MS Word to do all of our invoicing and then manually entering it into QuickBooks. It was a nightmare, and it made it impossible to track anything. We didn't have a good process for tracking who had been invoiced and who had paid.

How smart was it then for this company to come along and present their story in this way? Accounting software is, I hate to say it, a pretty tedious sell. But instead of leading with features and functions of what it did, they took an approach that struck me right in my gut. And it worked, for me and many others. Everyone within their target demographic who hit that home page could relate. Now, had someone who was running a large company with 150+ employees visited their website, it wouldn't have resonated with them. It would have been out of align-ment with what that person's expectations were about accounting software. But they understood their audience and they spoke to me.

We've all landed on websites that are trying to be a million things to a million people. And in effect what that does is water down the message. You have to make choices and be clear on what you're all about so your best customer can instantly relate.

CONCLUSION

You have a vision for why you built your business, a problem that you've set out to solve with your product or service. So, use that as inspiration to tell a story to your customer in a way that resonates on an emotional level. This needs to be married with the vision your customer has for why they're looking to make a purchase. This owned space—your website—is your chance to tell the world what you're all about. You need to get this right before you try to do anything else, because ultimately all other efforts will come back to this. Align with the vision of your best customer and the vision you had for why you built your product. This needs to be clear right out of the gate. That is the primary purpose of your website. And if there's no alignment between what you're saying elsewhere, your social media presence, your AdWords, and your website, then you'll lose people. Your website shouldn't be a honey trap.

Your website is your first opportunity to build trust with your customers, even more so than your salesperson, your receptionist, or anyone else in your company. Clutter, confusion, messiness, a lack of structure, no clear path to where a customer should go next and what you do—all this stands in the way of building trust. It's a little bit like walking into an office in a strip mall where there are wires hanging down from the ceiling and crappy furniture in the waiting room. The receptionist isn't very nice, and she doesn't really have any interest in talking to you. A website gives off the same impression when it's not put together properly—it doesn't build trust. The website is a first impression that is absolutely invaluable.

The other thing that people aren't doing is testing to see what they're biggest fans or their best customers think. They're putting their website up there because they are interested in the next deal, the next prospect, the next person. But your customers are a really important pool of people whom you should be leaning on for feedback in order to make your website better.

➡ Align.

➡ Organize.

➡ Test.

CHAPTER 7

DON'T PROPOSE ON YOUR FIRST DATE!

Imagine this scenario: It's five years ago, and you need to recruit a new employee, but you aren't sure what your options are for finding someone. You ask some colleagues how they find people with very specific skills, and a colleague you trust suggests a name of a recruiting firm that specializes in finding the type of person and skill set you require.

So you go to their website and read some content. And because you have a very specific and immediate need, you call them. (After all, there's not much else you can do on their website. Remember, this is five years ago.) After a lengthy conversation trying to understand how they recruit and what it costs, you realize you don't have the budget for this solution, and you don't think this solution is for you. What happens next?

Now that you've raised your hand, the company in question starts emailing and calling you once a month. Even though you were polite in the beginning, you make it very clear that you are not interested. They keep calling, and they suggest a revised calling schedule every quarter. You firmly tell them, "No," but now you're on their list, and they keep calling.

CLOSING THE DEAL

Everyone has experienced a scenario like this at one point. It happened to us recently at Marketing CoPilot, despite the fact that we unsubscribed from the mailing list. Every person in the office communicated the same thing when they were on the phone, but they kept calling. What if the same company had called us in the fall to ask about our hiring plans, and when they received the answer, instead of calling again three months later to ask if we were ready to buy something, they had sent a template about budgeting for new hires? Or even better, what if they emailed us a best-practice guide on how to onboard new employees? Best yet, what if they sent salary research about what people are getting paid in 2016 for the types of roles we were considering? Then that would be content we'd connect with.

They could have sent useful information to me, as a manager, to see what mattered to me and where I was in my hiring process. Instead they were bugging me and the team about whether we were ready to buy. Useful content changes the conversation. It makes it about my customer and not about me.

But why are so many companies still cold-calling and working from the same old script? Being asked for your number on a website is a turnoff just as is being asked for your number too soon on a date.

It's because performance is measured on how many calls that person makes, and how many deals they close. But what if performance was measured on content that engaged people over the long haul? If customers weren't ready to buy, they were at least ready to keep talking because it was a useful conversation.

Many people who are single have that friend who says, "If I'm not married by the time I'm forty, you and I should get married." I've heard this from so many twenty-somethings. I've been married for twenty-five years, but I'm sure that if I was single at forty, I'd be saying, "There was that one friend who has always been around..." And why? Over the long haul that friend was interesting and didn't ask for anything. He or she was there whenever you needed help and support, and was easy to be with. The same thing applies when you're trying to build a relationship online.

Today's sales funnel is pretty simple:

1. "I like your value proposition, and you're helping me fix a problem I need to fix right now." These customers will do things through the buying journey that suggests they're ready.
2. "I like your value proposition. I don't need to fix this problem right now, but I may need to do it shortly or down the road." These customers are keeping you around because they may want to come back to you later.
3. "I don't like your value proposition, and I'll likely never solve this problem with you." These customers are not interested in your product or service.

At any time, people can move between categories based on the way that you treat them. The truth is, I could have a hiring problem two months from now, but I will never pick up the phone and call that recruitment company because of the way they treated me. All they wanted to do was keep bugging me and asking me, "Are you ready to buy? Are you ready to buy? Are you ready to buy?" They kept trying to propose on the first date—and when has that ever been a good idea, in business or otherwise?

When a customer is ready to buy, she will let you know by taking a specific path. While working with a client of ours, we discovered that their buyer journey was very purposeful. When a customer had watched more than one video on the website, she would visit the pricing page and then enter her email to access gated content via the company brochure. Once all of these steps had happened, we were pretty sure we were going to hear from her. We didn't ask for a phone number when she downloaded the brochure. We just asked for first name, last name, title, email address, and the company she was with. We had decent information about her, but no phone number, because that's a friction point online. The minute you get asked to give up your phone number, even if you're putting in a fake one, you know somebody is going to try to call you. Otherwise, they wouldn't ask for it.

So we knew that by the time the customer got to that place, entered that information, and downloaded the brochure, we would probably hear from her within a month. We tracked it. We then sent the customer a relevant blog post and another download two weeks later. Then we usually saw some kind of activity in the two weeks following that. We could tell, very specifically, that she would contact us based on the content that she had consumed. Once the customer had submitted an email address to download that brochure, she immediately went into our email list. From there, with the email tool we were using, we could see if she had opened the most recent blog post email campaigner. We had seen, in some cases, that she had come back to it three or four times. We could see that the customer had not only opened it, but had clicked through to come back and read it over several days.

I always remind people that while you may think you're selling to a company, at the end of the day you're selling to a human being. We're all wired to react when we first meet someone. Whether that first meeting is through a website, by hearing someone speak at an event, or by reading a really great article that someone wrote, we have an immediate reaction. If you push somebody too fast and too soon because you're trying to get something out of them, his defenses go up and he becomes suspicious. That's just human nature. You wonder why the company is making it about them and not about you, the customer, because as human beings, we want everything to be about us. It's just the way people are. We all care about ourselves, first and foremost.

When you push people too fast, too soon, because you want them to do something, or you're forcing them to take an action—whether that's in real life when you're dating or in your business world—you get a reaction. And when you push them, it's often not the reaction you're looking for.

It really comes down to building trust—and your website is a great place to do that. So now that you know not to push too hard to make the sale, there are some other tools you can use that will lead toward closure without proposing on the first date. And the biggest one is good content. This takes many forms, and it depends on the level of sophistication you're willing to commit to. First, figure out what's working. Figure out what your audience is responding most positively to. Then, slice and dice that so you can serve it up in all different ways.

Maybe they want to understand just what the offer is— luckily, there are lots of ways to present that kind of info. The Content Marketing Institute does this really well. Recently they had an offer via social media for a budgeting template illustrating ROI that you could point your boss to as a way to get him or her to agree to pay for you to go to the conference. What a smart way to connect with their audience. A marketing director could go to their boss and say they really want to go to this conference. When the boss pushes back about not having the budget to send them, they're already armed with this document that will help them answer that question. Now that's a company who really knows what's important to their audience.

But what about when you just really need to close? It all comes down to the buying cycle. For example, we talked to a lady who runs an incredibly successful business called Cubeit. Cubeit is portable storage. It's a metal container that you have delivered to your driveway or your house when you're renovating or moving. You can fill it up, and then they move it, take it away to store it, or you just leave it in your driveway while you're doing the renovation. It's a fantastic business model, and she's grown significantly. When I sat down with her to brainstorm about what she can be doing from a content perspective, she told me that the decision to rent a Cubeit container takes a customer about three days—that's not a lot of time to get to know someone.

That's where search engines, AdWords, and things like that come into play as a way to align the website with what people are looking for and where they are at in the buying cycle. There needs to be a clear, quick explanation of what the product or service is and why someone would want it, plus conversion points on the site, because a customer is probably not going to want to engage with a company if he or she doesn't need something right now. For example, there are certain opportunities where Cubeit probably doesn't need to create a relationship. The customer either needs it or doesn't. But the trick is to understand how to build awareness with your brand over the long haul.

Maybe the customer is trying to put a budget together for how much the total renovation is going to cost. He wants to factor this in, but he's really not going to do the renovation until a year from now. Or the move falls through, and he decides to postpone it for another year. There are always reasons why people are not buying, and the trick is trying to understand that. It really has to come back to the length of your sales cycle: the complexity of what you're selling and how much education has to happen along the way for a sale to take place. From there, you can decide how quickly or how slowly you need to make "the ask."

Real estate can be a tricky business because they all work on commission. So if they sell the house or help you buy the house, they get paid. If you're a real estate agent, it's hard to differentiate yourself in that model. It's hard to align your value proposition with where you think your potential customers could be. But there are ways to work within these challenges. Perhaps the solution is to stay in one geographic area and become the expert on that area. Or maybe you sell into a specific ethnic community that gets you the win. There are lots of ways within that pool for agents to differentiate themselves, but at the end of the day, there's stiff competition in that world. If somebody has never used an agent before or if she's new to the area, then she's having conversations with friends, looking at your site, and checking you out. But what happens if she says, "I like your value proposition, but not right now," and chooses to go with someone else? Now you're put back into the pool, where that buying cycle could now be five to ten years, if at all, before she decides to buy something again. Do you want to invest in that, or do you want to speed date?

CONCLUSION

As much as you want every person who visits your site to do a free trial, book a consultation, or pick up a phone and call you to start talking to you about your products and services, it's not realistic. A standard rule of thumb for success is 1 percent. If you have one hundred visitors to your site, only one out of that group is going to pick up the phone and call or dash off an email to you. And if the number is zero, then you have work to do.

If you do achieve 1 percent, what are you doing for the other ninety-nine who visit? You need to understand who they are and what they need. If they weren't meant to be there in the first place, you'll see that via your bounce rate. But for the people who are there because they want to be and they're just not ready to take action, there are other things at play. Instead of trying to propose on the first date (trying to get them to buy now), you need to invest the time and money to get to know them first.

Instead of just looking for immediate leads, you should be looking for long-term engagement with a list that you're building over time. Be careful not to jump the gun too soon by offering things that seem to be spam or that make you appear distrustful. There's nothing worse than a pop-up box flashing in my face, saying, "Ready to buy?" Or a countdown clock that says I only have a few minutes left to buy. You need to be careful how you sell because it's going to take an investment to truly build a long-term relationship.

→ Don't propose on the first date.
→ Build long-term engagement.
→ Avoid cheap gimmicks.

FIND WHERE YOU NEED TO BE, AND MAKE IT HAPPEN

• • • • •

FINAL WRAP-UP

Sometimes the most obvious answer is usually the right one. Stop trying to be everywhere. If you've been spinning your wheels trying to be relevant by being on every social media platform, by throwing money at every new way to get customers, or by trying new things willy-nilly, then you've been wasting your time and your money. Take a deep breath, because the answer is much simpler than you may have ever realized. Instead of trying to be everywhere, start thinking about where you need to be in order to make the biggest impact with your customer. Figure out what makes your company, your product, or your process ideal for your customer, and then communicate that. And once you've made a change to your strategy, start testing by looking at your data to see if it's working.

Version 1.0 of what we call the Internet—that initial generation of what it looked like when we first started putting our companies online via websites—has changed. Back then it was okay to just take the company boilerplate or brochure and throw it out there for everyone to see. It's not okay to do that anymore. Instead of rushing to get a bunch of things done, we all need to sit back and think about what is really going to matter for our business—and what is really going to matter to our customers.

In chapter 5 we talked about how having 40,000 followers on a social media site does not equate to sales. You need to know what those people are doing on Twitter or Facebook with the information you're giving them—where they're going, what they're connecting with, what they're reading—before they decide it's time to enter the sales funnel. Instead of trying to be everywhere, test those places where you can make a connection with your customer. The thing you can't be afraid of doing is failing. The faster you fail, the more you're going to learn to help you understand what to do next.

The toughest thing about this new era of online marketing and digital tactics is that we need to be able to fail and fail fast. It's going to teach us something about where we need to be next. If you just have that Facebook icon up on your home page because you think it's supposed to be there, that everyone else is doing it so you should too, but you never take the time to see how it's performing or what it's actually doing for you, then you're making a huge mistake. As we covered in chapter 2, you have to take the time to look at and understand your data. Once you do, if you discover no one is clicking on that Facebook icon, then you've failed at what you were trying to do—and that's okay! Take it down and figure out where you need to be instead.

I recently discovered that a client I'd recommended to remove their Facebook icon took my advice. This particular company has a pretty dated website but is really trying hard to change. When they heard my advice, something clicked: They realized that putting a Facebook icon on a log-in page had no value. They listened to what we had to say because it's common sense. They had been afraid to take it down because they thought it was supposed to be there. But when they took it down, what they quickly realized was that not having a Facebook icon didn't have one ripple effect whatsoever for their business.

They realized how important content was in their business process to their customers, so they started investing there instead of putting empty efforts into social media. They recognized where content was really important, and they crafted custom content for the people who needed it the most. Some people might say, "Well, gee, that sounds like an obvious thing to do—of course you should have good customer content." But you'd be surprised how long it takes some people to get there.

Here's the good news for you: By not being everywhere, you're going to have a heck of a lot more time to focus on those things that really matter to your customers. Over the years I'm sure you've heard or read lots of things about all these places you needed to be and all of the things you needed to be doing in order to make your business successful. And guess what? You can be doing a whole lot less. Trying to be everywhere just because the Internet enables you to be is not the best idea. You need to simplify your efforts, return to what you're good at, think about who you serve well, and get that right above all. Getting that right will lead you to the next thing you should be doing.

The Internet has changed everything. It has made us believe we can put up businesses faster, accomplish things faster, change business models, disrupt industries, and all with the click of a few buttons. And certainly the

Internet can help us do these things. But whether you're a one-person shop, have a team of ten, or have offices around the world, competition today is fast and instantaneous. There's always going to be somebody nipping at your heels, and there's always going to be another way for somebody to solve a problem. Regardless of what you do, and who you sell to, there's always going to be another option. The competition is without limit.

The reason this is so urgent and why you need to get your own backyard organized first is because the longer you wait, the more you'll fall behind. There still seems to be a mentality in the small business world that a website isn't all that valuable, that an online presence doesn't matter. These are the people who think that they'll just do a bunch of things and see if they work, and when they don't pay off, they'll just walk away.

People don't realize that a website is the new receptionist. It's the new "open all night" sign. It's the new salesperson. The modern-day salesperson is now comprised of your online strategy, your content, and your content marketing program. This isn't to say that you don't need salespeople once you've engaged somebody in the process, but the role that a salesperson used to play in lead generation has evolved. Companies need to embrace this because those who don't aren't going to be around much longer.

The way you've always done things might need to change in order for you to stay relevant.

I spoke to a family-owned business not too long ago that was in the process of shifting control over to their thirty-five-year-old daughter. Traditionally, they'd had salespeople in their sixties who were out selling to other people in their sixties. It was a one-to-one relationship sale. What the daughter realized is that once all these guys retire, she wasn't going to have a business anymore. She needed to learn how to sell online.

There's a generational shift happening. And yes, while there are still businesses out there who can get away with not having a website and not having a content marketing plan, they're probably not going to be able to get away with it five years from now. Suddenly the value of their business is going to be next to nothing if there isn't some kind of online strategy and web presence with a well-thought-out marketing campaign. Having these things really does add value to your business. But the longer you wait, the quicker you're going to be left behind.

There might be people who say, "Well, that's always been true. There's always the next thing." That was true when the industrial revolution came along and displaced every-body who was in the farming community. We went from

90 percent of our economy based in farming down to 5 percent. There have always been these major shifts, and we're right in the middle of one now—the technological revolution. If you don't participate, you're going to get weeded out quickly. People won't choose you. They won't trust you. They won't believe you. Buyer behavior has changed, and customers want to get to know you long before you know they're looking. If you don't have that presence to warm them up, they won't even put you on the short list.

At Marketing CoPilot, we have you covered. We are in the process of writing a new guide called "The Essential Guide to Better Content Marketing." It's a thirty-page how-to of everything business owners need to know, which we will couple with a series of online courses.

If you want to get started right now, go log in to your Google Analytics and see what's happened on your website in the last thirty days. Look at where people land and what content they consume. Pick up the phone and ask your best customer how he or she searches for products and services like yours, and where he or she would like to connect with companies online. Then go back and take a good, hard look at all of the places that you are today and whether they're returning a positive ROI to your business. Do you have a way to measure each of those channels that you're in? Are you getting the return that you've been expecting? Then think about the one thing you could do—whether it's an email campaign, a blog post, or a video—to test whether or not the topics you're talking about with respect to your business are performing with your audience.

LIGHT ON THE OTHER SIDE

Following this advice will mean big things for your company. The promise land of a successful content marketing process is a never-ending stream of prospective customers who can't wait to talk to you. Imagine you're the most popular girl at the dance, and everybody wants to dance with you because they enjoy your content so much. They think you've really thought through your strategy and that you provide useful and helpful information to people when they go looking for a product or service like yours.

There's no magic bullet, but when you decide where you want to be and where you want to play, you'll stop wasting money on things that aren't working, and you'll see growth and success. Just because you think you should be in a million places doesn't mean they're all going to equate to success. You're going to find out really quickly that just being there doesn't mean success. You have to focus not only on where you want to be, but where need to be. It's a direct reflection of your customers. When you're able to sort that out, you're going to find really quickly that you're no longer wasting money or wasting time. You'll find you're exactly where you need to be to connect with the right people at the right time.

EPILOGUE

· · · · ·

My amazing grandmother, Cecile Marie Gagnon, passed away in 2014 at the age of ninety-four. She left behind twenty different uses for the rubber boot, five different methods for mixing cement, ten different uses for the elastic band in men's underwear, and six grandchildren, seven great-grandchildren, and one great-great grand-child, all of whom have learned from her common-sense approach to life: If it moves, feed it; if it doesn't move, Javex it; and *you can't be everywhere.*

ACKNOWLEDGMENTS

· · · · ·

I wrote this book because of all of the amazing clients, colleagues, friends, family and entrepreneurs who have helped me over the last 30 years. Thank you for never missing an opportunity to teach and inspire.

Specifically, I want to thank the team at Marketing CoPilot: Claudette, Maureen, Suzanne, Suzy and Dave who have provided moral support and were busy getting the job done so I could write this. I want to thank all of our past and current clients, too many to list here but an incredibly important part of this process.

Thanks to my mentors and collaborators over the years: Andrew Ford, Margaret Hoffman, Dr. Richard Hook, Rhomney Forbes-Gray, The Honourable Pauline Browes, the Gagnon sisters and the Wiese clan.

Thank you to the team at Book in a Box, Mark Chait and Zach Obront and, especially, Nicole Cammorata who worked so diligently with me on the content. Her patience and guidance was incredible.

And to the people who make me happy to get out of bed every morning, my family—Susanna, Jackson, Macy, Audrey and Dylan—keep passing the open window.

And finally, to my best friend David Tarrant: Thank you! It's as simple as that—thank you, thank you, thank you.

ABOUT THE AUTHOR

MARIE WIESE is founder of Marketing CoPilot, a leading Canadian digital marketing agency that helps companies increase sales using digital and content marketing. She is also an Executive-in-Residence at the Innovation Factory, a keynote speaker, a mom and a writer.

Made in the USA
San Bernardino, CA
04 July 2017